★ HOW TO BE *The Greatest* LIKE ★
MUHAMMAD ALI

The Life & Times of **Muhammad Ali**: the **Rebel**, the **Rivals**, the **Revolution**

STEVE DAWSON

Marshall Cavendish Editions

Text copyright © Steve Dawson 2012
Cover concept: OpalWorks Pte Ltd
Cover design: TeamAsia

© 2012 Marshall Cavendish International (Asia) Private Limited

Published by Marshall Cavendish Editions
An imprint of Marshall Cavendish International
1 New Industrial Road, Singapore 536196

Other Marshall Cavendish Offices: Marshall Cavendish Corporation. 99 White Plains Road, Tarrytown NY 10591-9001, USA • Marshall Cavendish International (Thailand) Co Ltd. 253 Asoke, 12th Flr, Sukhumvit 21 Road, Klongtoey Nua, Wattana, Bangkok 10110, Thailand • Marshall Cavendish (Malaysia) Sdn Bhd, Times Subang, Lot 46, Subang Hi-Tech Industrial Park, Batu Tiga, 40000 Shah Alam, Selangor Darul Ehsan, Malaysia.

Marshall Cavendish is a trademark of Times Publishing Limited

National Library Board, Singapore Cataloguing-in-Publication Data

Dawson, Steve.
How to be the greatest like Muhammad Ali : the life and times of Muhammad Ali : the rebel, the rivals, the revolution / Steve Dawson — Singapore : Marshall Cavendish Editions, 2012.
p. cm.
ISBN : 978 981 4351 41 6 (pbk.)

1. Ali, Muhammad, 1942- 2. Boxers (Sports) — United States — Biography. I. Title.

GV1132.A44
796.83092 — dc23   OCN796893517

Printed in Singapore by KWF Printers Pte Ltd

CONTENTS

★

DEDICATION

——— CHAPTER 1 ———
"GET UP AND FIGHT SUCKER!"
The Greatest Career   6

——— CHAPTER 2 ———
"WE WERE NOT ANTI-CHRISTS"
Black Athletes in America   58

——— CHAPTER 3 ———
"WHAT'S MY NAME?"
Conversion to Islam   70

——— CHAPTER 4 ———
"YOU MY OPPOSER"
The Vietnam War   84

——— CHAPTER 5 ———
NEMESES
Ken Norton & Joe Frazier   94

——— CHAPTER 6 ———
GENIUS TASKED
George Foreman   108

——— CHAPTER 7 ———
GENIUS DELIVERED
The Rumble in the Jungle   114

——— CHAPTER 8 ———
NEMESES AGAIN
Ken Norton & Joe Frazier   154

——— CHAPTER 9 ———
OLYMPIC REDEMPTION
The Greatest Love   170

ABOUT THE AUTHOR   198

PHOTO CREDITS   200

Dedicated to the late Harry Mullan, former editor of Boxing News, who read my undergraduate thesis, *The Economics Of Boxing*, and brought me ringside to report alongside him.

CHAPTER 1
"GET UP AND FIGHT SUCKER!"
★ The Greatest Career ★

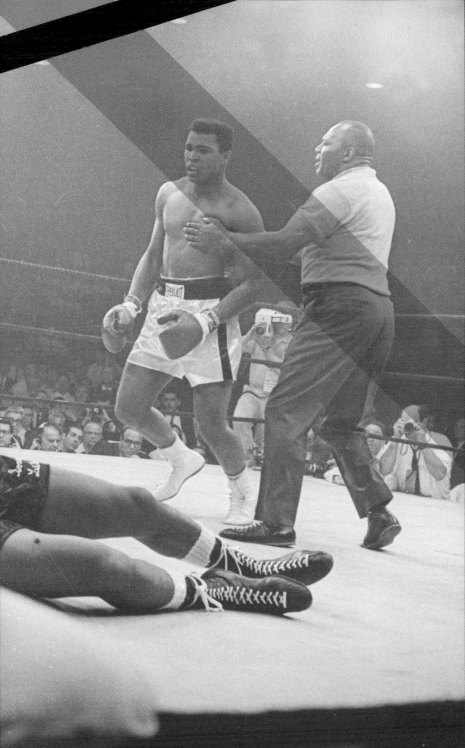

★ ORIGINS ★

He may be in his 70th year, surrounded by the happiness of a loving family and not short of a dollar or two, but Muhammad Ali's origins don't exactly make for happy reading. The same can be said of many African Americans some 450 years ago.

As early as the 1560s, African men and women were captured in their native territories and imported for sale to work as slaves, in what is now the United States of America. In areas where soil was at its most fertile, the system spread rapidly. Human labour was needed to harvest cash crops such as tobacco, cotton, coffee and sugar.

Between the sixteenth and nineteenth centuries, an estimated 12 million Africans were shipped to the Americas for enslavement, 645,000 of whom were brought to the United States. Factoring in children who were born into slavery, plus slaves originating from other parts of the world and Native American communities, by 1860 the United States Census reported a slave presence numbering four million.

In the early 1800s a farmer named General Green Clay returned from military duty to tend his land, an estate that made him the wealthiest man in Kentucky. As a landowner, he was also a slave owner. His son, Cassius Marcellus Clay, became a prominent anti-slavery campaigner.

Traditionally, slaves took the name of their masters. One such family worked on the Clay plantation for six generations. In tribute to Cassius Marcellus Clay's work in gaining their freedom, when that family welcomed a son in March 1876, they named him after the abolitionist.

He danced, played the piano and wrote music.

The boy grew up to become a billboard painter, but his artistic nature also shone through in other ways. He danced, played the piano and wrote music. In the 1930s he married Odessa Grady, whose paternal grandfather was a white Irishman. When Odessa gave birth to a son in Louisville, Kentucky, they too named him Cassius Marcellus Clay.

This boy, born on January 17th 1942, later became more popularly known as Muhammad Ali — or The Greatest.

★ THE EARLY YEARS ★

In October 1954 when Cassius Jr was 12 years old, he attended an annual convention at the Louisville Service Club. Cassius arrived with his friend on a shiny new $60 bike and went into the black merchant bazaar to take advantage of the free popcorn and ice cream. When they came out, the bike was gone. Tearful and as mad as an aggrieved 12-year-old can be, Cassius was directed to a policeman in the auditorium's basement. When he found the cop, he blurted out the whole story and vowed to undertake a state-wide hunt for his bicycle and the perpetrator before giving the thief a painful reminder not to touch what wasn't his.

The cop, Joe Martin, asked Cassius if he knew how to fight. "No, but I'd fight him anyway," Clay is said to have replied. He didn't know it then but at his life was about to take a tumultuous turn; from a young black kid in Louisville, to one of the most recognised men on the planet. Martin manned the local boxing gym in that very basement and invited Clay to come for lessons before getting himself involved in any challenges that he might later regret.

Martin went on to become young Cassius' trainer and stayed with him for the six years of his amateur career. Martin's wife Christine used to drive Cassius and other young amateurs for miles to tournaments in the area and even as far as Indianapolis and Chicago. She would go into the whites-only restaurants to buy them cheeseburgers and generally be as involved as her husband in all areas except training.

According to Christine, Cassius was the best behaved of all the boys; always obedient, polite and carrying his bible. Under Joe's tutelage and Christine's care, Cassius later enlisted the help of trainer Fred Stoner, who worked at the local community centre. With this backing, Clay compiled an extensive amateur record, the precise details of which remain subject to some debate. It's thought that Clay fought just over 100 fights, of which he lost only a handful. On the *Jack Paar Show* in America in late 1963, when asked how many fights he'd had, Clay replied with the merest hint of a smile, "About 108 amateur fights, lost 3, my first 3 by the way." Research indicates that his first bout was a victory over Ronnie O'Keefe in Louisville on 12 November,

1954, at age 13, with his first loss coming less than three months later in a Louisville Novice Tournament, against a boy named James Davis.

On 30 August, 1957, Clay beat Jimmy Ellis only to lose their rematch on a split decision the following month. Ellis would go on to win the World Boxing Association (WBA) heavyweight title in a round-robin tournament 11 years later. He would also lose a pro-fight to Clay in 1971 in a North American Boxing Federation (NABF) title bout.

★ 1960 ROME OLYMPICS ★

Having won national titles as a light heavyweight, including the Golden Gloves at 175 lbs in 1959 and as a heavyweight in 1960, Clay fought in San Francisco at light heavyweight in the 1960 Olympic trials. He had tried to make the grade at heavyweight but in the process lost to Percy Price of the Marine Corp. Price went on to win the heavyweight bronze medal in Rome but never turned professional, extending his career in the military instead.

At the Rome Olympics Clay fought at the light heavyweight limit of 81 kg (178.5 lbs). In the final he beat Poland's Zbigniew Pietrzykowski, who had been the bronze medallist four years earlier in Melbourne. At the time, Pietrzykowski was at his peak, having won the gold medal at the European Amateur Championships in 1955, 1957 and 1959. Pietrzykowski would go on to win again in 1963 and also capture the 1964 Olympic bronze, losing only to Laszlo Papp, who went on to win a third gold medal.

After his Olympic success, Clay immediately turned professional with trainer Angelo Dundee, a 30-year old who had already plenty of experience with former world welterweight champion Carmen Basilio and was

OLYMPICS
1960

in the Italian's corner when he beat the great 'Sugar' Ray Robinson for the world middleweight title.

In stark contrast to some of the venues he would fight at in years to come, Clay won his first fight the following month at the Freedom Hall State Fairground, Louisville. Weighing in at 192 lbs, he won a unanimous 6-round decision over West Virginia's Tunney Hunsaker who had a 15—9—1 (15 wins, 9 losses, 1 draw) record. At 30 years old, Hunsaker had seen better days, having lost his last six contests, including a decision to Ernie Terrell, who would go on to fight Clay amid great controversy in 1967 (see chapter 3).

Clay registered his first professional knockout two months later on 27 December against a novice named Herb Stiller in Miami Beach. This was only Stiller's third pro fight, having already lost once. Stiller would later also have Ernie Terrell on his career record, losing to him twice, the second time via a third round KO. Clay beat Stiller via a fourth round technical knockout, meaning the referee stopped the contest without having counted him out.

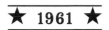

★ 1961 ★

In 1961, Clay fought eight times, winning them all while weighing between 188 and 195 lbs. The first four wins came via stoppage, with Donnie Fleeman taking him furthest, into the seventh round. Before stopping Fleeman, Clay had been winning the fight by a wide margin on the judges' scorecards. His performance was enough to end Fleeman's well-travelled career in which he'd stopped former world champion Ezzard Charles, albeit at the end of Charles' great career.

To this point, all of Clay's fights had either been in Louisville or Miami. His fifth fight of 1961 was his first in the bright lights and excitement of Las Vegas, a clear points win over Duke Sabedong, the first time he'd been extended to ten rounds.

A month later he would go ten rounds again. This time, against Alonzo Johnson, the scores were much closer — a sign of things to come when Clay's accurate fast hands would split judges' opinions when up against fighters who threw more punches but landed infrequently thanks to his excellent evasive techniques. Before meeting Clay, Johnson had won and lost decisions to future world light heavyweight champion Willie Pastrano and dropped a decision to Zara Folley, who would later fight the greats of the era, including Ali. Clay beat Johnson in a 50—44, 48—45, 48—47 10-round decision.

After two inside-the-distance wins to round off 1961, Clay embarked upon 1962 with a record of 11(8)—0 (11 wins, 8 by stoppage and zero losses).

★ 1962 ★

The following year started with a degree of panic and ended with the notoriety that Clay's camp was looking for. In February he took on Sonny Banks, a well-muscled American who had won 10 of his 12 fights. Banks' body shape was similar to Ali's. Both stood at 6ft 2in, and like Clay, Banks had fast hands. He was unranked, while Clay had already been promoted to number 9 in the highly-regarded *The Ring* magazine rankings. Banks was aggressive, yet cautious. All the signs from the opening moments pointed to the Detroit-based fighter being an intelligent boxer. Early in the first round he played the usual role of Clay's opposition, that of predator, as the more nimble Clay circled, banging in left-right combinations and deftly ghosting in and out of range.

One attack from Banks had him miss wildly with a swinging left hand as Clay effortlessly moved outside the attacking arc. Banks' momentum, having made contact with nothing but the cool air of Madison Square Garden in New York, saw him stumble embarrassingly towards the corner. Clay turned in towards him seamlessly and started to unload with both hands, looking for what would have been an impressive first-round KO on his debut in New York. The sixth punch he threw was a right hand in a downward arc towards the crouching Banks. It made contact but was nothing more than a glancing blow. As Banks came up for air, Ali's right glove remained in no man's land, providing balance for a follow-up left hook-upper cut. But just as the blow began its forward thrust, Banks fired off a left hand with impressive speed. It was all arm, with little evidence of the textbook transfer of body weight behind it. But such was its speed that Clay hadn't seen it coming and as it landed right on the chin, he instantly sank backwards and down to the canvas. It was what boxers call a 'flash' knockdown, where the fighter is less hurt than stunned. Clay got straight back up to receive the first mandatory 8-count of his professional career — it wouldn't be his last.

That was all Clay needed to realise that he ought not to hang around unnecessarily. After knocking Banks down in the second round, Clay dominated the third, landing with almost every punch as Banks' assault melted. The final minute was one-way traffic. Clay landed at will with rapier-like movement and the fight was almost stopped as Banks sunk to his stool at the end of the third. Sure enough, referee Rudy Goldstein needed only 26 seconds of the fourth round to decide that it was no longer a contest and a wobbly-limbed Banks was done for the night.

Despite the win, the story of the Banks fight had clearly been that Clay was floored. Could he take a punch? Was it just a flash knockdown? Why was he caught so easily by such a novice? Unsurprisingly, Clay's camp wanted to move on quickly and only 18 days later in Miami, he was back in the ring to register another fourth round stoppage against Don Warner. Two years later, Warner would suffer a first-round knockout by Sonny Banks.

A third consecutive fourth-round stoppage followed in May against George Logan, a man who had also beaten Ezzard Charles. 26 days later, Clay beat Billy Daniels in the seventh thanks to a cut that had opened up as early as the second round. It was time to step up in class and the two fights scheduled for the end of the year would achieve that.

Alejandro Lavorante had knocked out Duke Sabedong and Tunney Hunsaker, both in the fifth round. He'd also finished Zara Folley — a future Ali opponent — in seven and won a decision over Alonso Johnson. Crucially, he had also fought former world light heavyweight champion Archie Moore and although he had lost, Moore was the man being lined up for Clay's final fight of that year. Moore had scored a technical knockout in the tenth and final round against the Argentine, but Clay had Lavorante counted out in half the time. That lined up a match against his first world champion, albeit a light heavyweight and one who was just shy of his 48th birthday.

The fearsome World champion Sonny Liston attended the match in Los Angeles and entered the ring to shake hands with both boxers before the fight. Clay started mouthing off as the champion shook his right glove with both hands. Liston, smiling but without the skills to compete with the craziness that Ali could add to the hype, declined to get involved and walked across to greet Moore instead. Clay was making a habit of predicting the round in which his fights would finish and this prediction (a fourth-round stoppage) was getting more publicity than any other.

Moore exhibited the cross-arm defence that Ali would later face in three fights with Ken Norton, but the aging ex-champion would prove nothing like the pain in the side that Norton would, quite literally, be several years later. Moore barely threw a punch, so wrapped up was he in defending himself from the fast hands of the dancing Clay, whose youth and enthusiasm were far in excess of anything Moore could offer. Years later, Clay would find himself in a similar position again Larry Holmes and Trevor Berbick. But that was close to 20 years into Clay's future and about as conceivable as it had been for Moore when he'd begun his career 27 years earlier. Clay knocked Moore down three times in the fourth, standing over him after the first knockdown with his arms aloft, doing what would later become known as the 'Ali shuffle'. When the referee stopped the contest, both men embraced warmly, although the sight of Clay having lauded it over a great boxing veteran hadn't endeared him to everyone. Still, Clay had an important scalp and 1963 would be the home stretch in his march towards a crack at Liston's world title.

★ 'ENRY'S 'AMMER ★

In mid-March, seven weeks after knocking out Charlie Powell in three rounds, Clay took on New Yorker Doug Jones, who had just knocked out Zara Folley in the seventh and former light heavyweight world champion Bob Foster in the eighth, having floored him several times. Jones took Clay the distance for the fourth time in his career. It was a good workout at Madison Square Garden before a trip to London for his first overseas contest against the British and Commonwealth Champion, Henry Cooper.

With tongue firmly in cheek, Ali told a television news reporter, "I'm not training too hard for this bum. Henry Cooper's nothing to me, if this bum goes over five rounds, I won't return to the United States for 30 days, and that's final!"

Cooper was a solid-punching left-hook merchant — a punch, which by the end of Clay's career, would prove one of his few weaknesses. Cut and in danger of being stopped in the fourth, Cooper countered a clipping Clay left hook with a far stronger version of his own. The bell rang to save Ali, although he would have beaten the count. Far more dazed than he had been when Sonny Banks decked him, Clay made it to his corner, where his trainer Angelo Dundee orchestrated one of the biggest controversies of Clay's career (see The Greatest Mysteries — Clay vs Cooper I), extending what should have been a one-minute break to what Cooper remembers as being two-and-a-half minutes.

The replacement of an apparently ripped glove gave Clay more than enough time to get his head together and when he came out for the fifth, there was a far greater sense of urgency. Clay worked on the cut, knowing it was his best chance to get out of the fight intact. Ringside commentator Harry Carpenter described the action:

"Cooper's left eye is pouring blood. Gumshield's flying out, Henry is spitting blood. I think (referee) Tommy Little will have to stop this because Cooper's eye is really in an absolutely appalling state. It is the worst cut eye I've seen in a very, very long time indeed. I do not see how he can let this go on much further. And now he's stepping in and I think this is it. The towel has come in from Cooper's corner!"

– HARRY CARPENTER

★ BATTLING BRITS – HENRY COOPER ★

Google an image of Henry Cooper and you'll probably find that even though it's in black and white, there'll be an awful lot of red. Cooper was a popular British boxer and a famous British bleeder thanks to fragile skin that became increasingly susceptible to cuts, as scar tissue formed and re-formed around his eyes. His thinning hair and punished face seemed to always make him look like a senior citizen in the ring, although he was only 29 when he fought Cassius Clay in 1963. Look below the face at his hard, pale torso however and you'll see an athlete who had the conditioning to fight all night and the power to stun the world's best, if only he could get the job done before his skin would give way.

The British, who famously love an underdog, still love him today as 'Our 'Enry' — ex-national sporting hero turned loveable celebrity, even in his 70s.

During his fighting career, he almost always seemed to dominate the British and European scene but when asked to take that one final step towards the World Title, he seemed to fall just short. After a first-round stoppage of fellow Brit Brian London propelled him to greater things, Cooper was stopped in five rounds by future World Champion Ingemar Johansson in 1957. A year later he had recovered sufficiently to beat rated American Zara Folley on points, although he was stopped in their 1961 rematch within two rounds.

It was the following year in which he stunned Cassius Clay, felling him with a glorious left hook in the fourth, only to succumb to his vulnerable skin in the following round. Three years later, Clay, now World Champion and having changed his name to Ali, stopped Cooper in six rounds and it was largely downhill from there. Floyd Patterson stopped him in the fourth round four months later and after a swan song of seven wins on the trot, a young Joe Bugner came along and took his titles in a controversial decision.

All the while, Cooper had been winning the hearts of the British public in a series of fights with fellow Brits Brian London, Joe Erskine and Dick Richardson. Perhaps it was the failure to make the final step amid such tenacity that so endeared him to the British public.

He was knighted in 2000 and accordingly is now known as Sir Henry Cooper, or simply Our 'Enry.

★ CHAMPIONSHIP CHALLENGE ★

The world heavyweight champion was what, for many, a world heavyweight champion should be — tough, hard-hitting and intimidating. Sonny Liston was an ex-convict and an imposing character. His dark side was never difficult to perceive and his alleged connections to the underworld lingered well beyond the mysterious circumstances of his death.

Fifteen months before Liston defended his title against Clay, he had brutally pounded the popular and much smaller champion Floyd Patterson into submission inside the first round and repeated exactly the same thing in an ill-advised rematch nine months later.

As a churlish character, Liston was not a popular champion but with such a big mouth, many viewed Clay as even less likeable. Although Clay would weigh 20 lbs more than Patterson had for his first fight with Liston, the challenger was still a rank outsider with bookmakers as a 7—1 underdog. A *The New York Times* boxing writer named Joe Nichols declined to even cover the fight, thinking it would be a mismatch. Undeterred, Clay took to gate-crashing Liston's training camp, yelling at him and calling him a big ugly bear. Liston had neither the wit nor the inclination to compete with Clay's barracking. His mood on such occasions varied from amused to surly.

The fight took place in Miami Beach, Florida and when the boxers came together for the pre-fight instructions, it was obvious that Clay was the taller man, while Liston was thicker through the body and stronger.

Clay opened with frantic movements, even for him, darting his head in and out of range, lacking the smoothness that we'd seen before but with high energy, confusing the less nimble champion. He danced and flung out jabs, even displaying comparable strength in pushing Liston away when they got caught up from time to time.

Clay wasn't only concerned with jabbing from outside Liston's range. Rarely, but significantly, he unleashed with familiar two- and three-punch hooking combinations, especially when Liston would over-reach from the waist up and leave himself exposed.

In the fourth round Clay was masterful, circling Liston who held centre ring, firing single jabs into Liston's face, causing swelling around the champion's eyes and outscoring him handily. A reminder of Liston's threat came inside the final minute as he landed a firm right, followed by a thudding left. Unfazed, Clay continued to circle and ended the round with a flush left hook just before the bell rang.

Between the fourth and fifth rounds, a foreign substance that had fallen onto Liston's glove found its way into Clay's eyes. The precise nature and source of the substance has never been identified but some think it was the liniment used by Liston's corner to ease the pain in his shoulder that would later be significant in the fight's conclusion. Others say the substance had earlier been applied to Liston's eye injuries. That explanation seems to make little sense though because if it was so damaging to the eye, why would it have been used by the champion's corner on their own fighter?

There are also claims that the substance was intentionally placed on Liston's glove to hurt Clay. Years later it has been reported that Clay was offered a yellow substance by a stranger before his fight with Larry Holmes, which was claimed to temporarily blind his opponent. It was refused, but it made him think back and wonder about what happened on this night.

As he came out for the fifth Clay's eye was stinging, leaving him unsighted and asking for the fight to be stopped. Clay left his corner amid some panic, with Dundee having flushed as much water into Clay's eye as he could using a sponge, before pushing him out of the corner but warning him to stay out of Liston's way.

Television commentary described the first 10 seconds of the round with urgency, suspecting that a turning point was approaching:

"His eyes, his eyes are bothering him. Ladies and gentlemen, we don't know exactly what happened. They're yelling from Cassius Clay's corner. Something got in his right eye. However he's blinking badly!"

As Clay tried to run, Liston caught up with him and set about hammering the challenger's body with crushing blows. Clay seemed willing to take the punishment, burying his head on Liston's shoulder while holding the champion's neck to prevent a head attack.

Clay continued to back away. Survival was his only ploy now. Gone were the jabs; his hands were only used for defence and to paw at his eyes in an attempt to wipe away whatever foreign substance had breached his eyelids. Midway through the round, Liston tried desperately to land upstairs. He succeeded several times as Clay back-peddled, using his evasive instincts to lean back and take the sting out of Liston's punches as they landed. In retreat, Clay resorted to resting his outstretched left glove on Liston's forehead. At least then, even as a blind man he knew where his opponent was and having the longer reach could try to keep him out of range. Only in the final minute did Clay's eyes seem to clear, ending the round with some fire-fighting jabs before the bell gave his corner another minute's work at regaining his vision.

By the start of round six, Clay's eye problem had eased significantly. He was sticking and moving again, catching Liston's face at will, circling fluidly and scoring well.

As Liston sat in his corner after the sixth, it was apparent that something was amiss. Ice bags were applied to the champion's right eye in an attempt to arrest the rapid swelling, while a towel and some repair work were needed for a cut below the left eye. Liston's seconds were also aggressively massaging his left shoulder.

Clay was off his stool early for work in the seventh and raised both arms, engaging the 'Ali shuffle' a second before the bell sounded. Liston, though, was still engulfed by his handlers and as the referee strode over to hurry them away, one turned to him in apparent surrender.

Clay, now in centre ring, turned to his corner, clenching his fists above his head before bringing them down to his waist, yelling in triumph. His close second Bundini Brown ran towards him and hugged him around the chest, while Dundee, slightly more cautious, waited for a formal declaration. The referee strode over and raised Clay's hand, signalling the start of celebratory chaos. The new champion tore from one set of ropes to another, dragging his clinging entourage behind him. Without actually saying anything, his mouth was locked wide open, a pointed barb at journalists who had tagged him as a big mouth without the game to back it up. Those same journalists at ringside were treated to an I-told-you-so moment, hitherto unmatched in sports history.

The next day, the new champion changed his name to Cassius X and the following week, he became Muhammad Ali.

Officially, Liston had retired on his stool, citing an injured shoulder. A stoppage on cuts, which Liston certainly was struggling with, is a far more legitimate way for a fight to finish. An injured shoulder leaves the impression that the better fighter may not necessarily have been the eventual winner. A rematch made obvious sense and after a postponement so that Ali could recover from hernia surgery, the fight was set for Lewiston, Maine, the following May.

The next day, the new
champion changed
his name to
Cassius X
and the following week, he
became
MUHAMMAD ALI

★ POETRY - I AM THE GREATEST ★

"I am the Greatest! By Cassius Clay!" — Circa 1964

This is the legend of Cassius Clay,
The most beautiful fighter in the world today.
He talks a great deal and brags indeedy,
Of a muscular punch that's incredibly speedy.
The fistic world was dull and weary,
With a champ like Liston, things had to be dreary.
Then someone with colour, someone with dash, brought
fight fans a-running with cash.
This brash young boxer is something to see
And the heavyweight championship is his destiny.
This kid fights great, he's got speed and endurance
But if you sign to fight him, increase your insurance.
This kid's got a left, this kid's got a right,
If he hits you once, you asleep for the night.
And as you lie on the floor while the ref counts 10,
You pray that you won't have to fight me again.
For I am the man this poem is about,
The next champ of the world there isn't a doubt.
This I predict and I know the score,
I'll be champ of the world in '64.
When I say three, they go in the third,
So don't bet against me, I'm a man of my word.
If Cassius says a cow can lay an egg, don't ask how,
grease that skillet!
He is the Greatest.
Yes, I'm the man this poem is about,
I'll be champ of the world, there isn't a doubt.
Here I predict Mr Liston's dismemberment,
I'll hit him so hard, he'll wonder where October 'n
November went.

When I say two, there's never a third.
Betting against me is completely absurd.
When Cassius says a mouse can outrun a horse,
Don't ask how, put your money where your mouse is.
I am the Greatest!

★ 1965 ★

It was a tiny arena but one that would host a huge slice of
boxing history. As the bell for the opening round sounded,
Ali darted across the ring and cuffed Liston around the ear
with an opening right hand. Two seconds later he landed
another single shot, this time the left. Ali circled clockwise
with his hands below his waist, full of energy but this time
he retained the fluid style we were used to seeing. Liston
landed a jab as the two came together and Ali sent back
another left hand.

Around Ali went, still clockwise, offering his unprotected
head as target practice for the challenger. Liston leapt in
with a jab that was beaten away by Ali's defence. Still Ali
circled, foxing and faking as Liston paced forward and
sideways to track the champion's movement. Single and
doubled up jabs from Liston fell either side of their target.
Then Ali threw a left-right. It's unclear if they landed but
the ringside commentator described the right as "the best
punch thus far landed by the champion".

Ali continued to circle and Liston threw jabs that fell well
off target. Without deviating from his clockwise motion,
all the while moving away from Liston's powerful left hook,

Ali danced and bounced. Looking to back Ali into a corner, Liston threw another ineffective jab. It fell six inches short and a little beneath Ali's chin. Countering instantly, in a tight arcing motion, Ali lifted his right hand from below the waist and cut it across Liston's path at broadly head height in harmless-looking fashion. Liston stumbled forward and down onto his hand and knees before rolling over onto his back with his hands outstretched above his head on the canvas. Ali stood over him, resisting the advice to take a neutral corner and appeared genuinely furious, shouting, "Get up and fight, sucker!"

Liston now rolled over onto his front. He made his way up onto his left knee, with his right glove supporting him on the canvas and his left foot planted as if about to stand. But after holding that position for two seconds, he rolled over onto his back again, with his hands dramatically outstretched above his head. By this time, Ali was jumping around the ring with his hands in the air.

When Liston finally got to his feet, referee and former heavyweight champion Jersey Joe Walcott brushed Liston's gloves on his shirt and checked with ringside officials about the status of the count. Liston had been down for 16 seconds. Although the count is technically not supposed to start until the standing fighter retreats to a neutral corner, a ten count is officially enough to have registered a knockout. Without giving any instruction to the boxers, Walcott turned his back on the boxers to communicate with ringsiders and Liston and Ali resumed fighting, with Ali throwing several unanswered blows.

Watching the events unfurl from ringside, Nat Fleischer, editor of *The Ring*, took it upon himself to step through the ropes and advise Walcott that Liston had been down for more than 10 seconds and that the fight should be stopped. Walcott was also told by officials that they had already counted to 12. Either way, Jersey Joe figured there was little option but to end the fight. Amid chants of "Fake! Fake! Fake!", Ali had defended his title for the first time, but the question of whether he had beaten a man intent on losing would be debated for years to come and never resolved.

Ali's only other fight in 1965 came against Floyd Patterson, the man Liston had twice demolished for the title. That Ali could only put the former two-time champ away in the twelfth round at the Las Vegas Convention Center wasn't open to the obvious comparison with Liston's victories. That's because Patterson refused to call Ali by his new name and in referring to him as Cassius Clay, enticed Ali, not for the last time, to draw out a straightforward contest, prolonging the challenger's doom. Ali was well ahead according to all three judges, failing to win only two rounds on two scorecards and one on the other.

★ POETRY - THE EIGHTH ROUND ★

As read on the *Jack Paar Show* Circa late 1964:

"Ladies and Gentlemen for those who will not be able to see the Clay Liston fight, here is the eighth round exactly as it will happen.
Clay comes out to meet Liston and Liston starts to retreat,
If Liston goes back an inch farther he'll end up in a ringside seat.
Clay swings with a left, Clay swings with a right,
Look at young Cassius carry the fight.
Liston keeps backing but there's not enough room,

It's a matter of time and Clay lowers the boom.
Then Clay lands with a right, what a beautiful swing,
And the punch raises the bear clear out of the ring.
Liston's still rising and the ref wears a frown,
But he can't start counting until Sonny comes down.
Now Liston disappears from view, the crowd is getting frantic
And our radar stations have picked him up somewhere over the Atlantic.
Who on Earth thought, when they came to the fight,
That they would witness the launching of a human satellite.
Yes the crowd did not dream, when they laid down their money,
That they would see a total eclipse of Sonny."

★ 1966 ★

Ali's first full year as champion was a busy one. Although he had the linear claim to the world title (as traced by *The Ring*), his mission was to fight Ernie Terrell, the champion as recognised by the WBA, so as to unify the title. By now though, Ali was declining his draft to the Vietnam War effort and as a result, the Chicago State Commission refused to sanction the fight, so Ali went abroad to fight Canada's George Chuvalo in his hometown of Toronto, Ontario. Despite having to withstand a punishing body attack from the slightly heavier man of Croatian parentage, Ali ultimately won a unanimous 15-round decision.

Ali stayed overseas for much of the year. Next he met Henry Cooper in a rematch of their controversial 1964 fight. Again Cooper's cut-prone skin caused the stoppage, this time in the sixth round at Arsenal Football Club's then home of Highbury in London.

Still in London, this time at Earls Court three months later, the appropriately-named Brian London was outclassed by Ali in three rounds, before German fighter Karl Mildenberger suffered a twelfth-round TKO in Frankfurt just 35 days later.

Back home on 14 November, Ali met the big-punching and big-muscled Cleveland "Big Cat" Williams, in what some say was Ali exhibiting his peak. They are probably right. Even before the bell rang, Ali's energy level was noticeable. The ring announcer's interminable formalities were no reason for the champion to take a break as he danced all around the ring and shadow boxed with eye-catching thrusts. With the Vietnam controversy (see chapter 4) also at its peak, Ali was booed when announced to the audience. But unmoved, the champ gave those gathered a performance to treasure once the bell rang.

With beautiful poise, Ali glided around the ring, but this time with an intensity and solidity. For all his musculature, Williams was, at 33, a plodder and circled in centre ring as Ali bounded clockwise around him. The champion's utter command was soon evident with the 'Ali shuffle' (called so by the television commentator, despite referring to the champion as Cassius Clay throughout) occasionally thrown in even as both fighters were toe-to-toe.

In the second round, Ali's feet were proving that his head was far too elusive for Williams' fists. So much so that he even took to planting those feet and evading the challenger's attack by leaning out of range from the waist up. With 40 seconds left in the second, a blistering left-right sent Williams to the canvas. The challenger got up

Ali stood over him, resisting the advice to take a neutral corner and appeared genuinely furious, shouting,

"Get up and fight, sucker!"

quickly but a thudding combination that finished with a devastating left hand sent him down again. With less than 10 seconds to go, a powerful left-left-right sent Williams down again, only to be saved by the bell. In the modern day it's unlikely that the fight would have entered a fourth round and there was little point to it doing so in 1966. Belatedly, referee Harry Kessler called a halt to the fight in the fourth as Ali finished his man in the most electrifying style he had exhibited to date.

With Ali in this kind of form, fight fans were licking their lips at the prospect seeing him fight again. Sadly however, he would fight only twice more before we were all robbed of his talents for a barren three years and seven months. Three months later he beat Ernie Terrell in a one-sided, arguably cruel fifteen-round contest (see chapter 3) and then beat the aging Zora Folley, knocking him down in the fourth before stopping him in the seventh. It was here though, that Ali's refusal to be drafted as a soldier in the Vietnam War would disrupt the greatest of all careers, at its peak.

★ 1970-71 ★

When Ali's enforced absence from the ring was over, he fought an unsanctioned bout against Jerry Quarry to make his comeback in October 1970. He followed that third-round TKO with a 15-round stoppage of Argentine Oscar Bonavena.

The whole boxing world shaped itself for Ali's attempt to become the first man to regain his heavyweight title since Floyd Patterson. The 1971 fight at Madison Square Garden against Joe Frazier is one of the most famous in boxing history but it ended in a dramatic loss for Ali (see chapter 5). His return was set back significantly. As thrilling a fight as it was, Ali had lost for the first time in his professional career and the emergence of Olympic Champion, the immense George Foreman (see chapter 6), had also removed some of the heavyweight division's dependence on Ali's marketability. For the next 24 months, he would have to fight impressively and often. Rising to that challenge, he fought 11 times.

The North American Boxing Federation (NABF) title was vacant and Ali first met the far lighter Jimmy Ellis for the belt in July 1971. Ellis had grown up in Louisville with Ali, claimed an amateur victory over him and they had sparred thousands of rounds together. He had previously held the WBA crown and with Ali's permission, had Angelo Dundee (the trainer they shared) in his corner. Ellis though, despite knowing Ali's approach as well as anyone, couldn't recover from a counter right hand that he took in the fourth and lost by stoppage in the twelfth and final round.

Buster Mathis was next. Towards the end of his career, Mathis was hardly in the shape of his life at 256 lbs, some 20-30 pounds heavier than in his better days. The fight went the distance but Ali dropped his opponent twice in the eleventh and twice in the twelfth, easily outpointing Mathis and retaining the NABF title.

A month later on Boxing Day he knocked out German Juergen Blin in Zurich, Switzerland. Ali sauntered until the seventh round when he turned things up a notch before Blin's corner threw in the towel.

★ 1972 ★

A non-title fight followed in Tokyo, Japan, against another former sparring partner, Mac Foster. Ali was paid well to travel and this was never going to be a worthy contest for him — not everyone who attended would have been delighted with the lacklustre unanimous fifteen-round decision. 1972 hadn't started with a spark and the year, albeit busy, was lacking inspiration.

In May, a rematch with George Chuvalo (this time in Vancouver, Canada) for the NABF title again went the distance with Ali winning unanimously. The following month, another rematch against Jerry Quarry in Las Vegas once again ended early, this time in the seventh. Yet another pedestrian outing saw him beat Al Lewis in Dublin, with an eleventh-round stoppage, having scored a knockdown in the fifth.

In terms of getting in the conversation, as Frazier and Foreman hurtled inexorably towards one another, Ali wasn't really making an impression. Yes, he was beating all before him but who was he fighting and how convincingly was he winning?

A big-name fighter was needed and an aging Floyd Patterson provided that. He was clearly past his best, had already been beaten by Ali and during the exile years, Patterson had also been beaten by Jimmy Ellis. But, such as boxing is, the prospect of two former legitimate world champions attracted attention and 17,000 spectators filled Madison Square Garden to see both men surprisingly energised — Patterson by the prospect of a final shot at the big time and Ali by the pre-fight presentation of Joe Frazier in the ring to greet the crowd.

Patterson was surprisingly sprightly in the early rounds but at 37 he couldn't compete once Ali took charge, before stopping the old-timer in round seven.

Just two months later, Ali took on another much smaller man. He had outweighed Patterson by 30 lbs and in light heavyweight world champion Bob Foster, Ali now had a challenger who was over 40 lbs lighter. Foster was also four years older and had already floundered badly in the heavyweight division, losing by a second-round knockout to Joe Frazier. But he was coming off a triumphant fourteenth-round win over Britain's Chris Finnegan for the light heavyweight title at the Empire Pool, Wembley in London. It had been voted *The Ring*'s Fight of the Year and again Foster served as a respected opponent for Ali's resume.

Once again, Ali only got serious when an uncharacteristic cut opened around his left eye in the fifth. Not wanting to make scar tissue an issue of future fights, Ali let Foster have it for the rest of the round, knocking the challenger down four times. In the sixth he composed himself, dancing and circling and having steadied his hand, knocked Foster down again in the seventh before ending it in the eighth.

★ 1973-74 ★

Foster and Patterson had awoken the boxing world to the return of Muhammad Ali, although neither had been expected to present a significant threat. It was time to fight a legitimate heavyweight again and in February 1973, the European champion, Britain's Joe Bugner, was that man.

Bugner had beaten Brian London, Henry Cooper and on two occasions, Juergen Blin. At 219 lbs he was in fine shape and outweighed Ali by a couple of pounds. On a nine-fight winning streak, eight had come inside the distance and although Ali was favoured, he would have to work hard and box convincingly to win.

As it turned out, Bugner did his country proud. While never looking in great trouble, standing up to Ali and landing effectively, he seemed to lack the killer instinct to take advantage of his successes. When push came to shove, Bugner knew that Ali was stronger, quicker and more punishing and therefore held back cautiously, boxing within his ability. Ali won a comfortable 12-round decision and ironically, Bugner's next fight was against Joe Frazier. The Philadelphia-based fighter beat the Brit on points but had by now been dethroned by George Foreman.

Only a month after the Bugner fight, Ali hit another huge setback. He lost dramatically on points to Ken Norton before winning a hastily arranged rematch the following September. These matches gave fight fans some historic drama (see Chapter 5), which continue to be debated, as does their third and final fight in 1976 (Chapter 8).

Having avenged the second loss of his pro career, he needed to set right the first, by beating Frazier in order to get a shot at Foreman. Having dispatched Rudi Lubbers on points in Jakarta, a man Bugner had beaten before fighting Ali, Ali-Frazier II was signed for New York's Madison Square Garden, January 1974 (Chapter 8).

Ali's historic win finally got him another chance to wear the world championship belt with the famous 'Rumble In The Jungle'. Although Ali was not as sprightly as the days in which he fought Liston or Williams, he was now an experienced master of the ring, with uncommon endurance and the ability to soak up punishment with evasive manoeuvres. He also had a body that didn't wilt under pressure. His performance in Zaire against George Foreman was perhaps the most accomplished in all of sports and deserves special attention — see Chapter 7.

Ali was by now a two-time world heavyweight champion and appreciated as a boxer on a historic scale, one that transcended the sport to become the most recognisable man on the planet. As the champion again, the opportunities were there to once and for all right a couple of wrongs that had blighted his career, take his show on the road and get some paydays before leaving the sport for good with his health intact.

That was the plan, but it started unglamorously, defending his titles against Chuck Wepner in Richfield, Ohio. Don King promoted the fight and is reported to have paid Ali $1.5 million — a fine amount for fighting a journeyman prone to cuts. Ali coasted in exhibition style and later admitting that he hadn't trained hard, showed wonderful technique on his way to what he had probably accepted would be a points win (as had become his modus operandi in fights where he was clearly superior) until a punch under the heart saw him tumble to the canvas in the ninth. It seems clear from replays that Wepner (who was a bit of a clumsy fighter and had actually kicked Ali in the previous round, more through being off balance than viciousness) had stepped on Ali's foot, causing the champ to fall backwards.

Wepner later told a television chat show host: "I went back to my manager. I said 'Al (Braverman), start the car, let's go to the bank. We're millionaires.' And Al said, 'You better turn around. He's getting up and he looks pissed off.'"

Ali took the count in good spirits but made Wepner pay for his impudence in the subsequent minutes, worsening the cuts over his badly swollen eyes before the referee's tardiness was finally usurped by a 10-count, late in the fifteenth.

Less than two months later, Ron Lyle — a man who had done time for second-degree murder — gave Ali and his modus operandi a bit of a scare in only the third Ali fight to be broadcast live on home television. Lyle's tactics of patience and steadiness looked to be paying off.

But, behind on two judges' scorecards and level on the other, from nowhere Ali made scoring redundant with another one of those overhand rights sent in a downward arc in the eleventh round. With more back swing than the 'punch' that felled Liston, this one saw Lyle stumble into the ropes and was followed up by 44 unanswered blows. Ali even beckoned for the referee to step in, knowing that Lyle was too hurt to continue, but eventually Ferd Hernandez made his move and Ali retained his crown.

Since losing to Ali and then Joe Frazier, Joe Bugner had strung together eight wins, the last two by technical knockout. Mac Foster and Jimmy Ellis were among his scalps and he had also defended the European Heavyweight title thrice. The rematch with Ali would be in Kuala Lumpur, Malaysia on 1 July 1975. That it was a carbon copy of their first fight was dictated by Bugner more so than Ali. The sturdy Brit was able to defend himself capably as long as he didn't extend himself offensively. So, Ali bounced and jabbed his way to a comfortable 15-round unanimous decision.

On 1 October, Asia was also treated to the highly-billed Ali-Frazier III. The 'Thrilla in Manila' provided both men with the most physically arduous fight of their respective careers (see Chapter 8), but Ali wasn't ready to wind down yet.

★ BATTLING BRITS – JOE BUGNER ★

Jozsef Kreul Bugner was born in Hungary but fled as a boy with his family to the United Kingdom after the Soviet invasion of his country in 1956. His well-developed upper body and natural size meant that he excelled at school sports, winning the National Junior Discus Championship in 1964.

His breakthrough as a boxer came three-and-a-half years after turning professional when he challenged Henry Cooper for the British, Commonwealth and European Championship at Wembley, London. In accordance with boxing in that part of the world, there were no ringside judges and referee Harry Gibbs was the sole arbiter in deciding who should win the decision in a mightily close contest. Gibbs gave six rounds to Bugner and five to Cooper, with four even. Naturally it was hotly disputed and thanks to Cooper's popularity, was badly received by the press and public. BBC commentator Harry Carpenter famously protested on air: "How can they take away the man's titles like this?" Cooper retired, never to fight again.

"What saddens me most about the night I beat Henry is the way I was demonised afterwards. I was just a 21-year-old kid who came to fight," said Bugner in 2010.

"When Harry Gibbs raised my arm to signal that I had won, Henry said to him, 'I thought I nicked it', to which Harry replied, 'Son, champs don't nick anything' — and in boxing, that's the way it is."

"When Harry Gibbs raised my arm to signal that I had won, Henry said to him, 'I thought I nicked it', to which Harry replied, 'Son, champs don't nick anything' – and in boxing, that's the way it is."

Bugner's two fights with Ali, particularly the second, were characterised by his defensive tactics, turning the Kuala Lumpur contest into a snoozefest and prompting British newspaper *The Mirror* to call it "a monument to pacifism".

Bugner's finest hour came in the 1973 loss to Joe Frazier at Earls Court, London. In the tenth round Bugner was felled by a trademark Frazier left hook, but then showed the courage to get up and rally, hurting Frazier in the process. Harry Gibbs, again the referee and sole scorer, gave six of the twelve rounds to Frazier, with four to Bugner and two even.

"I was pissing blood for a week after that fight with Joe in London," Bugner recalls. "He was without doubt the most vicious fighter of that era and that includes Ali."

Bugner eventually moved to Australia and relaunched his career in Sydney with three wins over big names in the heavyweight scene — Greg Page, James Tillis and David Bey. That won him an opportunity for one last big payday in 1987 against Britain's Frank Bruno at White Hart Lane, home of Tottenham Hotspur Football Club. Bugner got battered on a night where the entire stadium seemed against him. Bruno had taken over the country's imagination, having lost bravely to Tim Witherspoon for the World Boxing Association crown a year earlier.

Sadly, eight years later he was back again, as a 45-year-old grandfather. The 1989 recession had made his vineyard investment a failure. His comeback was therefore a desperate attempt to recover some of that money. There was talk of a big fight with George Foreman but that never happened. He did win the Australian title and even a World title, albeit as deemed by the little known World Boxing Federation when James "Bonecrusher" Smith suffered a dislocated shoulder in the opening round of their 1998 contest.

★ 1976 ★

After such a historic battle, the champion took time out to toy with Belgium's hapless Jean Pierre Coopman in San Juan, Puerto Rico before finishing him in five. Two months later came an equally depressing points win over Jimmy Young in Landover, Maryland for another one-sided contest that saw Ali come in at 230 lbs, his heaviest ever. Twenty-four days later, as if to demonstrate how little he had exerted himself against Young, Ali took on Britain's Richard Dunn in Munich. The pale skinned, hard-hitting Yorkshireman got nailed with a thudding right hand in the fourth that sent a delayed message to Dunn's legs compelling them to give way. About a minute after Dunn had got up, Ali landed a similar single right, which staggered Dunn in a way rarely seen. His outstretched arms begged for stability like a tightrope walker on the cusp of falling. As he steadied himself, Ali — no longer punching — looked on, as did everyone at ringside, as if waiting for a dynamite-laden building to implode. As suddenly as he'd been hit, Dunn gathered his senses and sent out a southpaw right-left, hitting Ali whose guard was down watching in fascination along with everyone else.

Seconds later Dunn was decked with a peach of a right only to gamely find his feet once more. Dunn didn't really know where he was. Knocked down again, with one knee on the canvas, he hit Ali with a right hand. Ali stepped back while the referee started the count and lay on the ropes with his arms outstretched observing with fascination, how he'd been able to physically and mentally disarm a hard British man with the speed and accuracy of his punches.

Predictably it was all over in the fifth as Dunn went down twice more, again with almost cartoon-like delayed reactions, to Ali's right hands. It was an impressive reminder of what Ali could do to a heavyweight, even at 34 years old. But that Munich night would be the last stoppage win of Ali's career.

★ 1977 ★

After outpointing Ken Norton in their third and final fight (see Chapter 8), attrition and age were catching up with Ali. There is some evidence to suspect from television interviews that the early stages of Parkinson's disease, which would later severely curtail his movement and speech, was starting to settle in, as early as 1975.

The USA's Landover, Maryland, which had hosted the farcical Jimmy Young fight, was the similarly unfortunate venue for Ali's next opponent. Alfredo Evangelista's most notable opponent had been Rudi Lubbers and he'd lost his previous fight to Lorenzo Zanon. The Uruguyan showed little ambition and Ali coasted to another unanimous decision.

Ernie Shavers was another matter. His career knockout percentage of 92 (69 KOs in 75 wins) was already well in the making and although he had lost five fights, Ali's decline at 35 years old gave him an opportunity. Ali clowned before this fight as much as he had in the preliminaries of any other. By the second round Ali knew he could win a jabbing contest with Shavers but after unleashing an eye-catching flurry to a well-covered up challenger, Shavers came out of his shell and shook his head, waving his arms as if to say, "that didn't bother me". Seconds later Shavers sent a right-hand bomb to Ali's jaw, knocking him back into the ropes. Ali clinched in familiar style and glared at the crowd with his mouth wide open in mock shock. Shavers declined to follow up though and Ali built up a solid lead, giving some of it back in the championship rounds but doing well enough to win 9—5, 9—6, 9—6.

★ BATTLING BRITS - RICHARD DUNN ★

When Richard Dunn fought Ali in Munich in 1976, it was undoubtedly at the peak of his notoriety. Ali's performance then forced it into a dramatic freefall. Five months later he was KO'd in one round by the feather-fisted Joe Bugner, ending his career the following year with a stoppage loss, far off the beaten track in apartheid-ravaged South Africa.

"I was young, I was strong, I was fit, I was determined and I was the British, the Commonwealth and the European Champion, so I was entitled to be there," said Dunn, years afterwards in a television interview.

On that fateful day as Dunn made his way to the ring to face Ali, commentator Reg Gutteridge summed up the prevailing analysis of what was to come, by referring to Britain's unsuccessful attempts to prevent World War II: "Some cynics say that he's got as much chance here as Neville Chamberlain had in Munich in 1938."

At least Dunn had a puncher's chance, for what it was worth.

"As soon as I went out and tried to chin him, I thought, 'I could have trouble here,' and I did," said Dunn.

"I thought he was a terrific person, a terrific person. He was a great athlete. He had so much confidence, it was unbelievable. He put bums on seats."

"If he'd have been a dustman (*a British term for trash collectors*), he'd have been the best dustman in the world, because that's the type of man he was — he had to be the best at everything."

"I got to know him. Once or twice I went out with him and enjoyed it. He was a nice chap. His parasites that lived with him, I didn't like, you know his hangers on."

A pragmatic Yorkshireman thrown in with a brash American made for some contrasting approaches to pre-fight press conferences. In many ways, these were more entertaining that the fight itself and without question more evenly matched.

In one televised encounter held in the Olympiahalle, Munich, Dunn sat on his chair next to the interviewer with Ali some ten metres away beside another journalist. Suddenly Ali got up from his chair and strode across to Dunn. Pointing a fist in the Bradford man's face, Ali bellowed out: "I am the champion and I am the greatest fighter of all time!"

Dunn, arms folded across his chest, leaned over to the interviewer then looked up and across the vast auditorium. And almost imperceptibly muttered, "This is a nice place isn't it?"

"If he'd have been a dustman, he'd have been the best dustman in the world, because that's the type of man he was – he had to be the best at everything."

★ 1978 ★

By now Ali's personal doctor and corner attendant Ferdie Pacheco had advised Ali to quit and declined to supervise his fights any more. Ali though, wasn't ready to say goodbye to boxing just yet, especially as the young, inexperienced 1976 Olympic champion Leon Spinks, was ready to provide a supposedly easy payday in Las Vegas.

The 24-year-old brother of future champion Michael Spinks had only had seven professional fights and had drawn one of those. But as an Olympic champion — as Patterson, Ali, Frazier and Foreman had been before him — he had marketability.

For the early rounds, true to his secret to success in so many recent fights, Ali bided his time. Covering up on the ropes, as he had in Zaire against Foreman, several differences between this night and the one in Africa were becoming apparent. Firstly and rather obviously, Ali was four years older; Spinks was smaller and lighter than Foreman, and better able to maintain the pressure for longer. This was the air-conditioned Las Vegas Hilton Hotel, not the sweltering African jungle, also making it easier for Spinks to keep coming; and finally, perhaps crucially, Spinks fought a more intelligent fight. Instead of employing Foreman's big-bomb tactic, he was far busier, landing on Ali's body in bunches and also (as Ali held his guard in front of his face) to the side of his head, mixing in driving uppercuts and piercing Ali's defence.

When, after having conceded the early rounds, Ali tried to fight his way back on to the judges' scorecards, he wasn't able to muster quite enough. Despite a spirited final round, the 15-round decision was very much in question. Reg Gutteridge commentating for the British

I am the
CHAMPION
and I am the
GREATEST
FIGHTER
of all time.

closed-circuit audience described the announcement of the judges' decision:

> **Master of Ceremonies:** "We have a split decision."
> **Reg Gutteridge:** "It's a split decision! Now which way is it going to go?"
> **MC:** "Judge Art Lurie scores 143—142, Ali."
> **RG:** "Ali gets the first vote."
> **MC:** "Judge Lou Tabat scores 145—140 Spinks
> **RG:** "A big margin, 130—135. [sic]"
> **MC:** Judge Harold Buck scores 144—141, the new [the ring erupts with noise that barely makes the rest of the announcement audible] heavyweight champion of the world, Leon Spinks.
> **RG:** "One of the greatest upsets in the history of the heavyweight championship... Those of you in the cinemas of Britain have been the comparatively favoured few, to have seen live, the end of a legend and the birth of a great and willing young fighter from St Louis, the no-hoper who no critic thought could win."

Knowing that Ali was ever closer to the end of his career, Spinks was so willing to give him a rematch that the World Boxing Council version of Spinks' title was withdrawn for refusing to defend against the number one contender, Ken Norton. Spinks had a reputation as a party animal and had run-ins with the police. In contrast, during the seven months between their first and second fight, Ali trained harder, losing three pounds while Spinks put on four.

At the Superdome in New Orleans, Louisiana, Ali completely changed his game plan, taking the centre of the ring and scoring punches, nullifying Spinks' attacks by pulling the back of his neck in and down. It was a thoroughly convincing win, with all three judges giving Spinks only four of the 15 rounds. Ali had become the first man in history to win the world heavyweight title three times.

★ 1979-81 ★

It took The Greatest another nine months to officially announce his retirement in June 1979. In May 1980 he made a sad and embarrassing comeback against a champion on his way to excellence, Larry Holmes. Having been almost carried to an 11 TKO loss, where he didn't win a single round, an even less wise contest was arranged 13 months later, against future world champion Trevor Berbick. Predictably, the Jamaican ended the most historic of boxing careers in ignominy, winning a 10-round decision 99—94, 99—94, 97—94.

★ THE GREATEST MYSTERIES – CLAY VS COOPER I ★

In Cassius Clay's first fight with Henry Cooper, the gamble of travelling to England for the cut-prone but heavy-hitting Henry Cooper suddenly looked like a huge mistake when Cooper nailed Ali with a savage left hook in the fourth round.

Saved by the bell, Clay looked dazed and vulnerable. But as he sat on his stool, Angelo Dundee spotted a hole in Clay's glove, giving the referee no option but to allow time for the gloves to be changed, buying his fighter enough time to clear his head and earn a stoppage on cuts in the very next round.

Speculation that Dundee had cut open the glove with a penknife was rife for years. Much later, Dundee settled the argument by saying that the hole had presented itself some time earlier in the fight but when Dundee needed to take advantage of it, he stuck his finger into the hole, making it worse and enforcing the extended time out.

★ THE GREATEST MYSTERIES – CLAY VS LISTON I ★

Nick Tosches' excellent biography, *The Devil And Sonny Liston*, supports rampant suspicions that Liston threw the first fight with Cassius Clay by retiring on his stool claiming an injury to his shoulder, with the following passage:

"A few days after the fight, there came to light a contract that caused no small amount of speculation. Long before the fight — the contract was dated October 29, 1963 — Inter-Continental Promotions, of which Sonny was a partner, had contracted with the eleven-man Louisville Group to purchase for fifty thousand dollars the rights to promote Clay's next fight after the Liston match. This was a staggering amount to pay for the future rights to a single bout by a fighter who was seen as facing almost certain defeat in his upcoming match with Liston."

However, Tosches also pointed out that Dr Alexander Robbins of the Miami Beach Athletic Commission announced that Liston showed evidence of a shoulder injury that was "sufficient to incapacitate him and to prevent him from defending himself". This announcement expedited the release of Liston's purse, which had been withheld due to suspicions that things were not all they should have been.

★ THE GREATEST MYSTERIES – CLAY VS LISTON II ★

Although replayed footage ends any dispute that Ali did connect with the punch that felled Sonny Liston in their second fight, what seems in grave doubt to this day is whether it was thrown with enough force to knock him down. Liston's display while on the canvas certainly seemed the stuff of amateur dramatics, while Ali's reaction in standing over him and yelling seemed to support the theory that Liston took a dive.

Ali has never publically supported that theory saying that it was his 'anchor punch'. But what has become more infamously known as the 'phantom punch' is widely regarded today as having not been enough to have put a man of Liston's bulk on the canvas. Whatever the truth and it appears that will never be known, Liston will forever be inextricably linked to the underworld. The mysterious circumstances of his death in which his decomposed body was found with drug paraphernalia, including heroin and syringes nearby, lends itself to suspicion that it may have been his ultimate undoing. Liston had a lifelong fear of needles and friends claimed that although a heavy drinker, he never dabbled in heroin.

★ ALI ON TOUR ★

Where Ali fought as a professional

Country	City	City count	Country count
USA			45
	New York	10	
	Nevada	8	
	Florida	6	
	Kentucky	5	
	California	5	
	Texas	4	
	Maryland	1	
	Pennsylvania	1	
	Maine	1	
	Georgia	1	
	Ohio	1	
	Louisiana	1	
UK			3
	London	3	
Canada			2
	Toronto	1	
	Vancouver	1	
Germany			2
	Frankfurt	1	
	Munich	1	
Switzerland			1
	Zurich	1	
Japan			1
	Tokyo	1	
Ireland			1
	Dublin	1	
Indonesia			1
	Jakarta	1	
Zaire			1
	Kinshasa	1	
Malaysia			1
	Kuala Lumpur	1	
Philippines			1
	Manila	1	
Puerto Rico			1
	San Juan	1	
Bahamas			1
	Nassau	1	
		61	61

★ If you have a bike, think about how angry you'd be if some unknown punk stole it while you were trying to eat an ice cream. Channel that angst and learn how to fight. The thief may never identify himself but if he does, don't hit him. Charter a plane and take him to your country estate.

★ Don't sweat the small stuff. Do just enough to overcome your less-able adversaries. You'll need all the energy you have to dismantle the foes who'll end up defining you. If you do get in trouble, accidentally rip a hole in your glove.

★ Consider the maxim: if something is worth doing once, it's worth doing three times. Fight the big battles three times (if they'll let you) and win the big titles another three times. And don't be too worried by the occasional setback — revenge is sweet.

CHAPTER 2

"WE WERE NOT ANTI-CHRISTS"

★ Black Athletes in America ★

Although it may have seemed like Ali was breaking new ground as a black man winning the world heavyweight title (and let's face it, there was still plenty of ground to break), the very first man to wear the coveted belt had done so 56 years earlier. That man was Jack Johnson, born of former slaves in Galveston, Texas, in 1878.

After Johnson came more black heavyweight champions as recognised by *The Ring*: Joe Louis, Ezzard Charles, Floyd Patterson and the man from whom Ali won the title, Sonny Liston. Each had battled institutionalised racism throughout their careers and overcome it in the most emphatic of ways.

Johnson though, was the first — a tall, shaven-headed man who had built up his rake-like frame with dumbbells and commitment. His achievement came after making multiple defences of the "world coloured heavyweight title". Although inter-racial matches were common, the world championship was a white man's domain. It was only after more than 5 years of defending his 'coloured' title, impressing with victories over the likes of former world champion Bob Fitzimmons and publically haranguing the then champion, Canadian Tommy Burns, that he finally got his shot in 1908. But he had to travel all the way to Sydney, Australia to make it happen.

An editorial in Sydney's *Illustrated Sporting* and *Dramatic News* accounted for how the change of venue made little difference in the attitude of a black man fighting for a white man's title:

> **"** Citizens who have never prayed before are supplicating Providence to give the white man a strong right arm with which to belt the coon into oblivion. **"**

Johnson was far bigger than Burns. Over six inches taller, he also outweighed the champion by 23 lbs. Such was the beating that Johnson dealt out and such was the dissatisfaction with which it was received by the 20,000 Australians at Rushcutter's Bay Stadium, that police stopped the fight in the fourteenth round. In this event, as had been agreed beforehand, instead of the more common no-decision, the referee rendered a verdict for the winning fighter and new World Champion.

Back home, it wasn't long before white America heard about the news of how the sky had fallen in, albeit down under. From Sydney, reporting for the *New York Herald*, Jack London wrote: "No Armenian massacre could compare with the hopeless slaughter that took place in the Sydney Stadium today." It had been a fight between a, "colossus and a toy automaton... a playful Ethiopian and a small and futile white man... a grown man and a naughty child."

White America was up in arms. Randy Roberts' biography of Johnson, *Papa Jack*, captures the mood of the times: "Concerned whites said it should never have taken place. (Former world champion) John L. Sullivan, who by now had quit drinking and become a moral crusader, said, 'Shame on the money-mad Champion! Shame on the man who upsets good American precedents because there are Dollars, Dollars, Dollars in it.'"

"The Sadness that these men felt could only be expressed in superlatives — greatest tragedy, deepest gloom, saddest day, darkest night. The race war had been fought. Armageddon was over. The Caucasian race had lost."

Johnson held his title for seven years until 1915 when he was knocked out in the twenty-sixth round by a huge white American named Jess Willard. On 10 June, 1946, he died in a car crash near Franklinton, North Carolina, after racing angrily from a diner that had refused to serve him.

Twenty-eight years after Johnson's triumph in Australia, another black American took his talents abroad, this time a track and field athlete named Jesse Owens. His destination was Nazi Germany for the 1936 Berlin Olympics where he embarrassed Adolf Hitler by taking away four gold medals.

Albert Speer's *Inside the Third Reich* notes that Hitler was "highly annoyed by the series of triumphs by the marvelous colored American runner, Jesse Owens. People whose antecedents came from the jungle were primitive, Hitler said with a shrug; their physiques were stronger than those of civilized whites and hence should be excluded from future games."

With the world watching and the increasingly powerful Olympic committee taking careful note, Hitler kept his most stinging comments for select audiences, convincing Owens that the world's condemnation of Hitler's attitude towards him was overstated. But what was perhaps more alarming was Owens' perception of Hitler's behaviour in comparison to his own leader back home in America.

"The Sadness that these men felt could only be expressed in superlatives – greatest tragedy, deepest gloom, saddest day, darkest night.
The race war had been fought.
Armageddon was over.

The Caucasian race had lost."

Jeremy Schaap's *Triumph: The Untold Story of Jesse Owens and Hitler's Olympics* quotes Owens as saying: "Hitler didn't snub me — it was FDR (President Franklin D. Roosevelt) who snubbed me. The president didn't even send me a telegram."

Just over a decade later in 1947, Americans of all races had come home having fought side by side in World War II. But the summer sport of baseball, said to be as American as apple pie, was still a whites-only club. Black players were confined to the Negro Leagues. Segregation had been maintained to that point thanks to gentlemen's agreement between owners. But when the owners of the Brooklyn Dodgers took the brave step of signing an extremely talented and likeable man named Jackie Robinson to their organisation in 1945, the 26-year-old sidestepped verbal abuse and death threats to eventually make his Major League debut in 1947. That year baseball looked beyond his colour and solely at his contribution, presenting him with the inaugural Rookie of the Year Award. He went on to win the National League's Most Valuable Player Award two years later.

Today, it is traditional that on 15 April, the anniversary of Robinson's Major League debut, all Major League players be allowed to wear the same number on their backs — Robinson's number 42.

Very slowly, but very surely, black athletes made their mark on professional sports in America, rising through inhibiting strata to find quarterback spots in the NFL and become starting pitchers in Major League Baseball. Before too long, more than mere athleticism was acknowledged. In 1966 Bill Russell became the first head coach of a team in the National Basketball Association when he took charge at the Boston Celtics. But in the modern day National Football League, it wasn't until 1989 that a black man became a head coach, as Art Shell took over at the Los Angeles Raiders.

This sluggishness to accept the African American community in sport and more importantly in society, reached another milestone at the 1968 Mexico Olympics with what has been called the most political statement in Olympic history.

A black American named Tommie Smith had won the 200m in a world record time of 19.83 seconds, a mark that stood until the Italian, Pietro Mennea, broke it at high altitude in Mexico City some 11 years later. Taking the bronze position in Mexico was another black American, John Carlos.

When the sprinters received their medals on the Olympic podium, they chose to attend the ceremony shoeless, wearing black socks — a gesture that they said represented black poverty. Smith wore a black scarf around his neck while Carlos donned a string of beads in memoriam of black people who had been lynched in racially-motivated attacks.

Much of this might have gone unnoticed, but when the American national anthem began, they delivered a gesture that became front-page news around the world. With their heads bowed, Smith and Carlos each raised a black-gloved fist to represent Black Power — not merely a protest but a showing of strength, resistance, perhaps even aggression.

They had planned to use a pair of black gloves each but Carlos had forgotten his and the silver medallist, a white Australian named Peter Norman, suggested that they share Smith's pair, wearing one glove each. Norman also went to the podium shoeless. He was later reprimanded by his country's Olympic authorities and, on his return from

If I do something good then I am AMERICAN, but if I do something bad then I am a NEGRO.

Mexico, ostracised by its media. He was not picked for the 1972 Australian Olympic team, despite finishing third in the trials. When Norman died in 2006, Smith and Carlos acted as pallbearers at his funeral.

Smith would later say of his times: "If I do something good then I am American, but if I do something bad then I am a Negro."

There was as diverse a reaction to using the Olympics as a podium for a political stand, just as there had been to Muhammad Ali's use of the World Heavyweight title in advocating his philosophy. But in this case, the timing was poignant in causing unease. Smith and Carlos chose the very moment that America was being honoured for contributing its athletes; the national anthem was being played before the world; and the Stars and Stripes were being raised in celebration. It was an extremely high-profile time to register their displeasure. Sure enough, what was seen as America's public humiliation at the way it treated a segment of its citizenry made both athletes marked men for years to come.

In an HBO documentary *Fists of Freedom*, Smith said: "We were not Anti-Christs. We were just human beings who saw a need to bring attention to the inequality in our country. I don't like the idea of people looking at it as negative. There was nothing but a raised fist in the air and a bowed head, acknowledging the American flag — not symbolising a hatred for it."

There is a feeling that Smith in particular has tried to downplay the symbolism of their gesture over the years, perhaps withered by the backlash they received. But the picture of both men is impaled upon sporting and cultural history and onlookers will make what they will of its imagery.

"We were not Anti-Christs. We were just human beings who saw a need to bring attention to the inequality in our country. I don't like the idea of people looking at it as negative. There was nothing but a raised fist in the air and a bowed head, acknowledging the American flag – not symbolising a hatred for it."

HOW TO BE THE GREATEST

★ Take inspiration from those who have come before you. Apply their strength of character to your own fight, in your own times. Take the right path and you'll be revered for what you fought for — with or without your gloves.

★ Be well-read about the history of your stand. If you can find a mentor to guide you, listen and learn. Be conceited like Jack, humble like Jesse, respectful like Jackie and in-your-face like Tommie and John. It takes all sorts.

★ Take your message to people around the world and unveil it only when you have their attention and respect. Tough messages may need a hard sell — timing is everything.

CHAPTER 3
"WHAT'S MY NAME?"
★ Conversion to Islam ★

Muslims have been immigrating to the United States in increasing numbers since the 1880s. Today, native-born Muslims in the US are mainly African Americans, who account for 24 per cent of all Muslims in the country.

Since the 1960s, prominent Americans in many walks of life have either converted to Islam or were born into the religion, many of them sporting icons. Six-time National Basketball Association championship winner Kareem Abdul-Jabbar converted just before his career started in 1968, while four-time champion Shaquille O'Neal is perhaps the most famous current player who is a Muslim. But perhaps more than any other sport, boxing continues to feature well-known Muslim Americans and their high-profile conversions.

In the 1980s, the light heavyweight division alone gave fans in the United States three world-champion Muslim converts. Two-time national amateur champion in the early 1970s, Eddie Gregory, changed his name to Eddie Mustafa Muhammad as a professional and won the World Boxing Association title in 1980. Although he defended the title twice, he lost it in 1981 to future heavyweight champion Michael Spinks (younger brother of Leon Spinks, who faced Ali twice, beating him the first time).

At around the same time, a boxer named Matthew Franklin, who had fought and lost to Eddie Mustafa Muhammad in 1977, was coming into his own. Franklin had won the WBC crown in 1979 and converted to Islam, changing his name to Matthew Saad Muhammad. He made eight successful defences, including two against popular British fighter John Conteh.

While Saad Muhammad was tall and rangy even for a light heavyweight at 5 ft 11, Dwight Braxton, the man who eventually dethroned him in 1981, was squat and thickset with seemingly invincible power and will. Braxton was only 5 ft 5 and had spent five years in jail for armed robbery. Braxton beat the champion with a tenth-round technical knockout and promptly converted to Islam, adopting the Muslim name Dwight Muhammad Qawi.

The following year he beat Saad Muhammad again, then made one more successful defence before losing to Michael Spinks.

These three did much to increase the awareness of Islam for 1980s sports fans. Journalists and fans were obliged to take their new names on board while the trio played musical chairs with the world title. This ensured that their faith remained in the public eye, not least of all because, between them, they helped launch the even more notable career of Michael Spinks.

Another man whom Spinks tussled with is Malik Abdul Aziz, better known as Mike Tyson. Spinks was made a 91-second martyr in 1988 with the World Heavyweight Championship at stake. Four years later though, Tyson was convicted of a rape charge and converted to Islam while incarcerated. In 2000, during a post-fight interview while gunning for a fight with the then World Champion Lennox Lewis, he famously said (and let's face it, rather incongruously for a man of faith):

"I'm the most brutal and vicious, the most ruthless champion there has ever been. No one can stop me. Lennox is a conqueror? No! I'm Alexander! He's no Alexander! I'm the best ever. There's never been anyone as ruthless as me. I'm Sonny Liston. I'm Jack Dempsey. There's no one like me. I'm from their cloth. There is no one who can match me. My style is impetuous, my defense is impregnable, and I'm just ferocious. I want his heart! I want to eat his children! Praise be to Allah!"

It was back in 1964 that Cassius Clay paved the way for these men to convert in the public eye without any mainstream backlash. It started when Sonny Liston failed to answer the bell for the seventh round of his world heavyweight championship defence against Cassius Clay. The new champ had things he wanted to get off his chest, and he wasn't backward at coming forward.

Ringside reporter Edwin Pope of the *Miami Herald* said: "I was so stunned. I was just electrified and there he was, right in front of me and a whole bunch of other newspaper men, pointing down to us, like this, 'I told you, I told you. I told you exactly what I was gonna do.' Well we were just sitting there stunned. We didn't know which key to hit first."

Ali would have berated the print media all night if he hadn't been interrupted in the ring by a television interviewer. But he wasn't about to let the man with the microphone set the agenda.

"I don't have a mark on my face, I upset Sonny Liston and I just turned 22 years old, I must be the greatest! I told the world!" The interviewer, apparently clueless about who it was that the world wanted to hear, tried to direct the performance. But Ali broke free: "I am the King of the World! I'm pretty! I'm a bad man! I shook up the world! I shook up the world!"

Nonetheless, the world wasn't aware quite how much more shaking there was to come.

As the new champion, Ali had a huge platform on which to announce his conversion to Islam. Less than a month into his reign, a television reporter asked him why he insisted on changing his name from Cassius Clay to Muhammad Ali.

"That's the name given to me by my leader and teacher the honourable Elijah Muhammad. My original name, that's a black man's name. Cassius Clay was my slave name, I'm no longer a slave."

"What does it mean?" asked the reporter.

"Muhammad means worthy of all praises and Ali means most high."

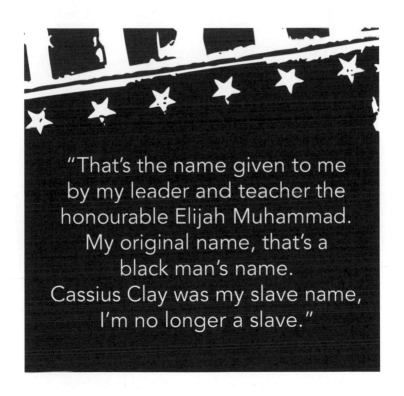

"That's the name given to me by my leader and teacher the honourable Elijah Muhammad. My original name, that's a black man's name. Cassius Clay was my slave name, I'm no longer a slave."

White, conservative America was unsettled by such talk. The world heavyweight championship belt was to be worn with pride. Boxing wasn't perhaps the most gentlemanly of sports but it carried some responsibility. The status quo was already being shaken by American liberals and the right wing response was becoming equally historic.

In August of the previous year, Martin Luther King had delivered his enduring, 'I Have a Dream' speech; barely three months before the fight, democrat and President John F. Kennedy had been assassinated; in July of 1964, five months after the fight, President Johnson signed the Civil Rights Act; while in February of the following year, the black nationalist Malcolm X was shot to death while conducting a civic meeting.

Three months after Malcolm X's death, Ali took a barrage of questions from the media. A composed and soft-spoken Ali was asked if his involvement in the civil rights movement would extend to the point of being arrested.

"No Sir. That's an embarrassment. I'm supposed to be free. I don't have to be getting locked up." He was then asked if his sobriety here meant that the loud-mouthed antics surrounding his fights with Liston were just an act.

"A wise man can act a fool, but a fool cannot act like a wise man," was his reply. "I'm a wise man."

Ali continued to defend his title, although, perhaps because of the angst he was causing at home, in 1966, he took his show on the road to Toronto, London and Frankfurt. In February 1967, almost two years after changing his name, Ali fought a 6ft 6, 27-year-old from Belzoni, Mississippi, named Ernie Terrell. In the media build up to the fight, the boxers were interviewed by veteran journalist Howard Cosell, who stood between them as the fighters stood face to face.

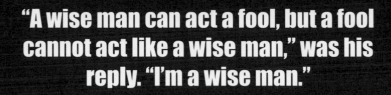

"A wise man can act a fool, but a fool cannot act like a wise man," was his reply. **"I'm a wise man."**

Terrell: "I'd like to say something right here. You know, Cassius Clay is..."

Ali: "Why do you wanna say Cassius Clay when Howard Cosell and everybody is calling me Muhammad Ali. Now why have you got to be the one, of all people, who's coloured, to keep saying Cassius Clay."

Terrell: "Errr... Howard Cosell is not the one who's gonna fight you. I am."

Ali: "You've made it really hard on yourself now."

Cosell, an excellent journalist who would strike up a friendship with Ali over the years, recognised the theatre that was unravelling, understood his role perfectly and kept a sharp eye on both players, shifting the microphone from one to the other, so that those watching wouldn't miss a word.

Ali: "Why don't you call me my name man?"

Terrell: "Well what's your name? You told me your name was Cassius Clay a few years ago."

Ali: "I never told you my name was Cassius Clay."

Terrell: "Well…"

Ali: "My name is Muhammad Ali and you will announce it right there in the centre of that ring after the fight, if you don't do it now."

Terrell: "For the benefit of this broadcast, him, alright. Err…"

Ali: "You are acting just like an old Uncle Tom; another Floyd Patterson. I'm gonna punish you."

Clearly lacking Ali's loquaciousness, Terrell transferred his weight from one foot to another and inched forward towards Ali.

Terrell: "Why you wanna call me a Uncle Tom?

Ali: "What you gonna do? You heard me! Just back off of me!"

Terrell: "Wait a second, wait a second. Let me tell you somethin'. You ain't got no business calling me… Don't call me no Uncle Tom man."

Ali (talking over Terrell): "Back off of me! Back off of me! That's what you are, an Uncle Tom!"

Cosell, aware that his audience might not be ready for what this was escalating into, interjected, or tried to.

Cosell: "And so ladies and gentlemen…"

Ali: "Uncle Tom!"

Terrell: "Wait a minute."

Ali: "Wait what. Back off of me man."

Those last five words seemed to come without the humour that usually accompanied Ali's rants. As they were uttered, he pushed Terrell hard in the chest and the meeting dissolved into a restraining exercise involving security.

When finally they fought in the ring, Ali did what he implied he would do — punish Terrell. But not by blowing him away in the early rounds. This fight went the distance. Not necessarily because it had to, but because Ali was in full control and wanted to draw out his opponent's agony and humiliation for the full 45 minutes. The eighth round was the most representative of all. Ali spent the first two minutes with his hands at waist height, in stark contrast to Terrell's high, peek-a-boo guard. Terrell threw jabs but almost all were off target as Ali relied solely on his reflexes, leaning back out of range and making no effort to use his hands for protection. Contrastingly, Ali's lightning-fast, stinging jabs penetrated Terrell's guard, causing swelling around the eyes.

The final minute saw Ali talk almost constantly to Terrell, "What's my name Uncle Tom? What's my name?" as he moved up a gear, sending left and right hooks to the challenger's head. At the bell, Ali stood in front of Terrell and again, without any of the usual sense of theatre, a furious Ali let his opponent have it, verbally, which may or may not have been a nice change for Terrell from the physical beating he had just taken.

In the break, Joe Louis, a black fighter and former world champion, for whom America had widespread respect, gave his thoughts to commentator Cosell. In doing so, Louis confirmed that the Champion's mouthing — inaudible to the television audience — had indeed been, "What's my name?" But poignantly, in a moment that reflects on Terrell's later pronouncement that his initial pre-fight faux pas had been a genuine slip, Louis also referred to the champion, not as Ali, but as Clay.

HOW TO BE THE GREATEST

★ Dare to be different if your belief system is different. Don't let anyone disrespect that difference, even if they've suffered a similar struggle to your own. Some people don't have the strength, education or understanding. Fight them, to fight for them.

★ Punish dissenting voices without mercy. Draw out their punishment, call them names, humiliate them publicly — all without the sense of humour that you might otherwise be known for (there may be some wiggle room here).

CHAPTER 4
"YOU MY OPPOSER"
★ The Vietnam War ★

The swirling and defining events of 1960s America were not just confined to Islam, civil rights and assassinations. The Vietnam War was also raging — a conflict that pitted North Vietnam and its communist allies against South Vietnam, supported by America and other anti-communist nations. As a poor South East Asian country became the battleground of the Cold War, it's thought that there were more than a million war-related deaths, with 58,000 Americans among those who perished.

Compulsory military service in the US came to an end in 1973, but conscription to fight in Vietnam, also known as the draft, was still a legal obligation for those unable to gain exemption.

Elvis Presley, who became as big a star in the music world as Ali would become in his profession, had already been subjected to conscription. In March 1958, "The King" reported to the Memphis Draft Board, swapping his blue suede shoes for army fatigues adorned with the serial number 53 310 761. Private Presley was sworn in and amid great media fanfare said his goodbyes to family members before getting bussed to Fort Chaffee, Arkansas, where he received that much-photographed G.I. haircut. To widespread hilarity, it was there that he employed (and some say coined) the phrase 'hair today, gone tomorrow'.

America was not at war when Elvis was drafted. He enjoyed considerable time with family and friends and even managed to squeeze in a Nashville recording session. This wasn't simply a public relations campaign for the army however. Elvis spent 18 months on assignment in Germany before being honourably discharged in March 1960. Asked in a television interview about the decision to place him in the field rather than in the entertainment service, Elvis replied:

"I was in a funny position. Actually, that's the only way it could be. People were expecting me to mess up, to goof up in one way or another. They thought I couldn't take it and so forth, and I was determined to go to any limits to prove otherwise, not only to the people who were wondering, but to myself."

Peacetime conscription is one thing, but when there's a war to fight, especially such a controversial one staged on the other side of the world, not everyone was as keen to take part.

In a 1977 interview with *High Times*, a magazine for cannabis users, guitarist and song writer Ted Nugent described his actions to avoid the Vietnam War draft: "I ceased cleansing my body. Two weeks before the test I stopped eating food with nutritional value. A week before, I stopped going to the bathroom. I did it in my pants. My pants got crusted up." Somewhat older, and presumably cleaner, he denied the story 29 years later in an interview with British newspaper *The Independent*.

Even the stars of Hollywood were expected to serve their dues, except actor George Hamilton, who was then dating one of President Johnson's daughters. He claimed draft deferment due to "extreme hardship" on the grounds that his mother relied upon him to care for her.

Canada was officially a non-participant in the Vietnam War. Canadian anti-war activists encouraged their American counterparts to head north. Some 'draft dodgers' were accepted by Canadian authorities as immigrants. It's estimated that as many as 125,000 Americans came to Canada because of their opposition to the War, with half of that number staying permanently.

Muhammad Ali wasn't heading north; instead he registered his stance on the Vietnam War with the media, labelling himself a conscientious objector. On 8 May 1967, Ali formally refused to be drafted into the armed services. By now he'd defended the world heavyweight title nine times. No matter, jail was now a possibility and being stripped of his heavyweight title and license to box a stark reality.

"Those who think I have lost so much by not taking the step, I would like to say that I did not lose a thing. Up until this very moment, I haven't lost one thing. I have gained a lot."

Five days after lodging his objection, Ali clarified his stance to a gathered audience. "Those who think I have lost so much by not taking the step, I would like to say that I did not lose a thing. Up until this very moment, I haven't lost one thing. I have gained a lot. Number one, I have gained a peace of mind. As you read the newspapers, you can see that I am now in court. I am in court, seeking justice under the laws of the land. In this country, the United States of America, ministers are exempt from the armed services. And, if they choose, I am a Muslim minister and a teacher of Islam."

Ali would spend years justifying this stance, but surely nothing he said in that time can be more persuasive than this statement, made in front of pressmen and the general public:

" I'm not gonna help nobody get something my negros don't have. If I'm gonna die now, right here fighting you. If I'm gonna die. You my enemy. My enemy is the white people, not Viet Cong or Chinese or Japanese. You my opposer when I want freedom; you my opposer when I want justice; you my opposer when I want equality. You won't even stand up for me in America for my religious beliefs and you want me to go somewhere and fight but you won't even stand up for me here at home. "

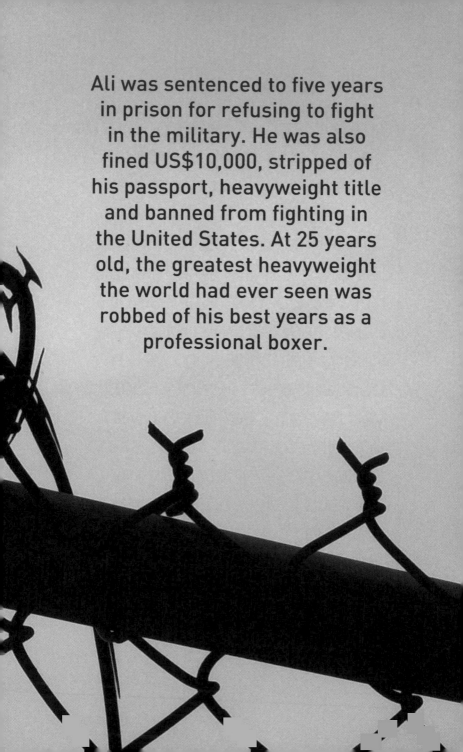

Ali was sentenced to five years in prison for refusing to fight in the military. He was also fined US$10,000, stripped of his passport, heavyweight title and banned from fighting in the United States. At 25 years old, the greatest heavyweight the world had ever seen was robbed of his best years as a professional boxer.

He was at least released on appeal but spent the next three years lecturing at universities and Muslim gatherings. His appeal reached the Supreme Court in 1971 and by an 8-0 ruling, Ali had his conviction reversed. He could fight again.

HOW TO BE THE GREATEST

★ Fighting for peace isn't always a contradiction. Pick your battles though. Choose your enemies carefully and your allies even more so. Be prepared for jail and even to die for your principles if you really are The Greatest. Study the law of the land and look for whatever loopholes may help you. Or pay someone to do that on your behalf.

★ Stay healthy and strong, because one day the world will see things the way you do. When that day comes, you'll need your strength to live, unbridled, in the way you've chosen.

------ CHAPTER 5 ------
NEMESES
★ Ken Norton & Joe Frazier ★

If we discount Larry Holmes and Trevor Berbick as boxers who beat Muhammad Ali when he was well beyond the peak of his abilities, nobody else can officially claim to have gotten the better of Ali over the course of their respective careers.

1976 Olympic light heavyweight gold medallist Leon Spinks managed a win and a loss against Ali and therefore might call for an honourable draw. To be fair though, he has never done that and nor has anyone else on his behalf. Ali lost to Spinks when he was a fading force at the age of 36 and Parkinson's disease, while still undetected, was already eating its way into his nervous system. Regardless, having lost to Spinks on a split decision, seven months later he took on the 25-year-old again and soundly outpointed him 10—4, 10—4, 11—4.

The only other men to defeat Ali were the athletic and opportunistic Ken Norton and the man by whom most analysts gauge Ali's greatness, Joe Frazier. Between them they fought Ali six times but never fought each other, although both were annihilated by George Foreman (see Chapter 4).

★ ALI VS FRAZIER I ★

The first of those six fights was in March 1971 at Madison Square Garden, New York City. Ali had already fought twice since coming out of his enforced exile, having scored stoppage wins over Jerry Quarry and Oscar Bonavena. Frazier had won the 1964 Olympic heavyweight gold and by the time Ali was temporarily banished from the sport, had fought as a professional for two years, stopping all of his opponents. In the time since Ali's exile, Frazier had won the world title and defended it six times, including a points win over Bonavena and a seventh-round knockout of Quarry.

Ali wore unfamiliar red trunks with white trim for this third comeback fight, while Frazier was decked out in an exotic green and yellow. Frazier was the shorter man, a shade under six foot, but his stocky thighs and a muscular, stout body packed immense power. Coupled with a relentless oncoming style, he made a ferocious opponent.

Typically, Frazier came out throwing punches almost without rest — he knew of no other tactic. Even Ali's ghost-like defence was occasionally exposed. Several times in the first few rounds, Ali would pull Frazier into his body, lift his chin and shake his head in denial that there was anything to Frazier's power.

Offensively in those early rounds, Ali was fresh and fired in swinging combinations. Frazier's defence was his offence. He crowded Ali, making him back off or cover up. By the final third of the 15-round fight, Frazier's face was distorted far beyond its normal appearance; puffy around the eyes and forehead, a swollen testament to Ali's persistent abuse.

Despite stopping 37 men in his career, the vast majority were from the accumulation of Ali's quick-handed combinations. He was not a big hitter in the true sense of the word and rarely finished fights with a single devastating shot. Ali unleashed in bunches, but on this night, his opponent wasn't succumbing to his consistent barrage.

On came Frazier, shuffling forward even if it meant he would eat Ali's leather. And then, in the eleventh round, Frazier's march paid off. A wide-arching left hook brushed Ali's face, for a second, seemingly shutting down all movement in Ali's body as he tried to gather perspective.

Advisedly, he sought to hold Frazier and bring him inside to reduce his opponent's leverage. Smokin' Joe slipped free and sent in a digging left hook to Ali's stomach, the next punch came back upstairs, without the backswing of the previous two. It was short, solid and landed flush on Ali's jaw. The challenger's knees collapsed and he sunk towards the canvas, rescuing the situation at the very last moment, energising those thighs to propel himself upright.

If it hadn't been for the ropes, Ali may well have gone down, but in jacking himself up, he also went backwards, finding the ring's border to give that extra support he desperately needed.

The round was far from done with 40 seconds left and Frazier pressed further. Ali tried to dismiss the moment by mocking Frazier, wide-eyed and mouth agape but he wasn't fooling anyone. With Ali looking like he'd escaped the worst, he panicked his corner again. Caught by a speeding left hook, he again clung for salvation but when Frazier slipped away once more, Ali's legs couldn't move as quickly as his brain had asked. Unable to move those feet in time to support his lurching body, Ali fell alarmingly into the ropes, clinging once more and buying just enough time for another minute's rest between rounds.

Reprieved, Ali continued to land punches but it was clear they didn't have enough to stop this steam-roller of a man. In the fourteenth, the Philadelphia fighter's will triumphed again. Ali sent an awkward left hand downwards to Frazier's gloves. It had started life as a left hook to the head but Frazier's movement saw Ali pull out at the last minute. Realising that it wasn't going to land, they came together in the confusion and Ali pushed his opponent away, regaining the distance he needed to try the same punch again. As he did, Ali saw an opening and pulled back his right hand to unload. In an instant, just as Ali was about to pull the trigger, Frazier skipped forward, transferring his weight and firing off a left hook of perfect technique and crushing power. It landed on Ali's jaw, breaking it. Ali fell to the canvas in the same arc as the punch had been thrown, if anything making it seem even more powerful.

Ali rolled over to his left side and got to his feet instantly. He survived the round without excessive trouble. Ali's jaw had instantly ballooned, making his pretty face ugly.

By the end of the next round, Ali's career was in the hands of the judges, who scored the 15 rounds unanimously 9—6, 11—4, 8—6, all to Frazier. Ali's comeback had hit a roadblock that he'd failed to get through.

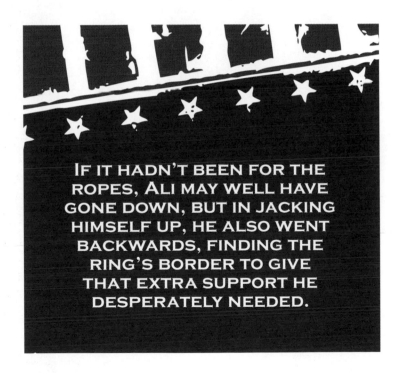

IF IT HADN'T BEEN FOR THE ROPES, ALI MAY WELL HAVE GONE DOWN, BUT IN JACKING HIMSELF UP, HE ALSO WENT BACKWARDS, FINDING THE RING'S BORDER TO GIVE THAT EXTRA SUPPORT HE DESPERATELY NEEDED.

Ali's jaw had instantly ballooned, making his pretty face ugly.

★ ALI VS NORTON I ★

Over the next two years, Ali fought ten times, trying to wipe the Frazier loss from his resume. He won all of them, six inside the distance. But only 44 days after going 12 rounds with the strong but ineffective Brit, Joe Bugner, he took on Ken Norton in San Diego on 31 March 1971.

Norton was an athlete in tremendous condition. A sculpted body with far less body fat than Ali, his slim waist and enormous shoulders didn't fit the standard look of a boxer. In the ring, Norton didn't run but neither did he chase Ali. Consequently, they stood toe to toe but that didn't mean they brawled. This was a chess match with high stakes, each looking for openings in a fascinating duel.

Norton wasn't a natural boxer. He threw punches in singles, with his eyes looking down, well beneath his target, leaving his head as an unprotected beacon. But although Ali connected, he couldn't put his man away. Norton had quick hands. He couldn't flurry like Ali but his jab and straight rights pursued and caught Ali's face like an attacking cobra, fracturing Ali's jaw as early as the second round. Angelo Dundee tried to have the fight stopped, but Ali convinced him that he could go on and win.

He was mistaken and stunned by a man who prior to this contest had fought nobody of note, earning only US$300 on the previous occasion he'd got in the ring. Ali was Norton's ticket to bigger things and he took his chance with both gloves. Injured and ill-prepared, Ali lost the 12-round contest on a split decision 6—5, 4—7, 4—5.

★ ALI VS NORTON II ★

From a results perspective, losing to Norton was the lowest point of Ali's career. His attempt to regain the heavyweight title, taken from him outside the ring, was now looking light years away. Losing to the Olympic champion Joe Frazier was something he could work towards correcting, but this loss to a raw, if gutsy, bodybuilder seemed a point from which a return looked bleak. The only way back was to avenge the loss straight away and Ali went into training for the rematch which took place later that year on 10 September.

Norton showed up in the same kind of crazy shape he was in for the first fight, but Ali had made an extra effort, shedding nine pounds to come in at 212 lbs, compared to 221 lbs for their first fight. That extra conditioning seemed to pay off. Ali came out dancing and stayed on his toes for much of the fight. Norton's unorthodox cross-arm defence was just another reason that he continued to look nothing like the natural boxer Ali was, but substance and not style were what the judges were after.

It was another bruising battle in which both men took punishment. By the end of the eleventh, Norton had started to show the greater wear and tear, weary of arm and leg, his heavy muscles were proving a dead weight compared to Ali's nimbleness — a characteristic he displayed even during the final twelfth round. Most had the contest too close to call, with those last three minutes the determining factor on many unofficial cards at ringside. After both fighters fell into an embrace as the final bell sounded, they retreated for the judges' cards to be totalled up.

Amid the usual post-fight chaos, Ali caught the eye of Howard Cosell coming into the ring to interview the winner. He still had time for some light-hearted fake hammer blows to Cosell's head while the announcer's back was turned. After that, Ali looked out over the top rope as the decision was announced.

Losing to Norton was the lowest point of Ali's career.

"Ladies and gentlemen we have a split decision," came the public announcement. It was close, not good news for Ali. Norton's honest, hard work, if lacking in finesse, had caught the eye again. But had it been significant?

"Judge John Thomas at ringside scores it 6—5, Ali."

Cheers gave way to muffled boos as the crowd fought to give their response. With his gloves and bandages cut away, Ali placed his forearms on the top rope and stretched out from the waist, looking weary. His head hung down towards the canvas. He knew that split decisions were read out with the deciding card coming last, so as to maximise the drama. The next announced score would be in Norton's favour.

"Judge George Latka at ringside scores it 6—5, Kenny Norton." Boos rang out overwhelmingly now as Norton, already with his blue gown on, poured water over his head. Across the ring, Ali maintained the same position, with his back to everyone else, still looking down.

"The deciding vote was cast by your referee Dick Young..." The television director had to make a call. Needing the winner's reaction to the decision and with a camera on both men, he cut to Norton.

> ## ... He sees it 7–5, to the winner – split decision: Muhammad Ali.

Norton shook his head in a resigned way, as if satisfied that he had at least done his best. Belatedly, the director switched cameras to Ali, whose hand was being raised by a member of his entourage.

Now, Ali could re-set his sights on regaining the world title. But a variable that made the process more complicated was now in play: Joe Frazier was no longer champion. To get to the new champ, George Foreman, he would have to fight Frazier again.

★ ALI VS FRAZIER II ★

Forty days after the Norton fight, Ali won a 12-round decision against Rudi Lubbers in Jakarta, Indonesia. Three months after that, he was scheduled to meet Joe Frazier for the second time. But five days prior to their New York fight on 28 January 1974, the whole event was thrown into jeopardy when the two got involved in a brawl at the ABC television studios. The confrontation, which saw both men grappling on the floor, was anything but staged. Ali had continued to refer to Frazier as 'Uncle Tom' and an 'ugly gorilla'. These terms cut deep with Frazier, who was being portrayed by the highly-effective Ali publicity machine as supported only by conservative white America. Ali, he would claim, had the love and support of his own

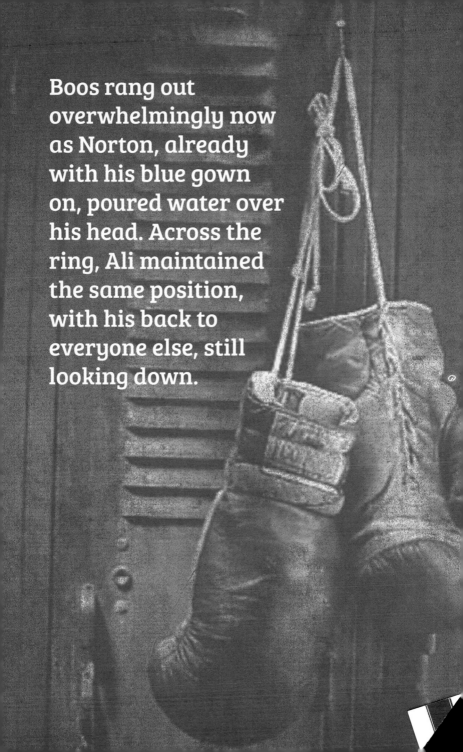

Boos rang out overwhelmingly now as Norton, already with his blue gown on, poured water over his head. Across the ring, Ali maintained the same position, with his back to everyone else, still looking down.

ethnic group and indeed, broad-minded white liberals. In the studio interview, the two suited fighters had got it on when Frazier refused to sit down after rising from his seat to put a stop to Ali's constant taunting.

For the fight they were being paid for, both men wore white. Weighing 212 lbs (identical to the second Norton fight), Ali came out light footed, executing perhaps the sweetest and most subtle version of the famed 'Ali shuffle' in his career as early as the first round. No matter how many times you see it, you wonder how a man with such a frame could make it look as if he was floating on air.

Ali moved, circled and floated, stopping only to plant his feet briefly for two-handed flurries to Frazier's head. Frazier, mindful of the 12-round duration, hunted his prey steadily with more pragmatic, economical footwork, looking for a chance to cut Ali off as he circled, enticing him to move into one of those blistering left hooks.

Fast forward to what are today known as the championship rounds, 11 and 12, and Howard Cosell reported that journalist Larry Merchant's scorecard had Ali so far ahead that Frazier needed a knockout to win. Merchant, it was also pointed out, had Ali ahead when their first fight concluded, although all three judges disagreed.

Frazier's movement remained identical to the first round, the only evidence of the nine rounds in between were his swollen eyes and forehead. Ali had reduced the dancing to a slow waltz but was neither exhausted nor desperate. He still circled but on the flats of his feet rather than his toes. He planted those feet purposefully, to find Frazier's head with both hands, but now he had to do that more often — dancing his way out of trouble was no longer so easy.

Frazier had shown little of the destructive power that characterised the first fight. Ali's feet early on, and later his fists, had prevented that. In the final minute Ali saw light at the end of the tunnel and brought out the flash. He flurried with exultation and even pulled off another Ali shuffle, this time with the speed but without that inexplicable floating illusion that he'd managed at the beginning of the night.

By the time the final bell rang, the announcement was made without any drama — there was little debate to be had. Ali won by a unanimous decision 6—5, 7—4, 8—4. In the ring, Frazier told Cosell that although he'd landed the most effective punches, he didn't have any arguments.

Ali said to Cosell: "I hope to go on, to get to the title and then get on out of this."

HOW TO BE THE GREATEST

★ Find a worthy opponent, a nemesis with the respect of those you seek to impress. Put on a show, build up the hype and back it all up with the substance of unwavering bravery in the face of broken bones, extreme exhaustion and unstoppable opponents.

★ Disregard initial failures. Have the patience to map out your path to redemption and navigate accordingly. If it helps, call your enemies 'ugly' and question their loyalty to your shared heritage.

CHAPTER 6

GENIUS TASKED

★ George Foreman ★

George Foreman was a monster.

At 6ft 3½ and 220 lbs, the 25-year-old had not only beaten but, like a human snow plough, had shovelled aside everyone they'd put in his path. His first professional fight was in New York on 23w June 1969 when he knocked out Don Waldhelm in the third round.

Over the remaining six months of that year, the 1968 Olympic champion embarked on a whirlwind campaign, propelling himself toward a title shot. On average, he fought once a fortnight. By 6 December he had amassed a record of 11—0 (10 KOs). His twelfth fight of that year saw him go 10 rounds for the first time against Levi Forte in Miami Beach. But while a fighter's first ten-round contest is a milestone to prove he can go the distance, for a knockout artist like Foreman it was a blot on his copybook. As if to right the "wrong", only two days later, on the other side of the country in Seattle, he knocked out Gary Whiler inside the first round.

The following year in 1970, he fought 12 times. Only one went the full 10 rounds. By the end of his fourth professional year, Foreman's record was an astounding 37—0 (34). In 1972, every single one of his five fights finished with his opponent being counted out in the second round.

Watching closely — with a bank account waiting to be filled — was Joe Frazier. Having beaten Ali in 1971 to retain the world heavyweight title, Frazier defended his crown twice the following year, beating little-known challengers Terry Daniels and Ron Stander, winning both by knockout. When finally the inevitable title defence against Foreman came around, the world would see the most devastating conclusion to a fight that perhaps it has ever known.

Frazier, the man who had given Ali his toughest fight ever, was dropped three times in the opening round and Foreman's devastating right hand was to blame. The second knock down had the Philly fighter in a distressed state of vertical collapse, like a skyscraper collapsing from explosives that had ripped out its foundation. Almost instantly he got to his feet, those thick, muscular legs transforming the 29-year-old athlete into a drunk, staggering across an otherwise empty Philadelphia bar.

In the second round another swinging right hand saw Frazier stumble across the ring, a pre-cursor to the break dancer who would only be seen on the street corners of Frazier's hometown some 10 years later. Humiliation was now in full effect.

But the American public already knew about Frazier's inhuman strength and desire. Here, it was to be his downfall. Straight back up, Foreman unleashed upon him. A vicious left hand had Frazier on the canvas for a fifth time. In modern times, the fight would surely have been stopped but on it went and on went Frazier, refusing to give up.

Finally, to the relief of every humane conscience, a short, powerful right, not quite an upper cut but delivered in a hooking upward arc, landed flush on Frazier's jaw. The reaction on Frazier's body was like nothing seen before or ever since. After the merest of moments, seemingly of realisation rather than reaction, Frazier's entire body was propelled upwards from the blow, his feet jettisoned from the ground. Nobody at ringside had seen a fighter, let alone one of Frazier's bulk, be lifted off the canvas by a punch. When he landed, simultaneously on his left knee and right foot, the referee — mercifully for everyone — stopped the contest.

Frazier had not only been beaten, he had been annihilated.

Foreman's sixth consecutive second round knockout had stunned the boxing world and it was followed up eight months later by a first round knockout defence against Jose Roman in Tokyo. Then, if he hadn't already done so, he sealed the deal by swatting the only other man to beat Ali, Ken Norton, taking less than two rounds in March 1974.

In light of the Frazier culling, Ali had laboured but nonetheless carved out revenge wins after initial defeats by Frazier and Norton, setting up the one fight that everyone wanted to see. The date was set for 30 October 1974, in Zaire.

One of the oldest truisms of boxing is that styles make fights and this was the classic brawler/puncher versus boxer/mover battle. Add to the promotional mix these ingredients: heavyweight boxers; a world title; in Foreman, a man that scared America, the most fearsome man since Sonny Liston; in Ali, the most charismatic man of the television era — a black man, a Muslim and a 'draft dodger', yet strangely irresistible — a man whose popularity was growing infectiously.

HOW TO BE THE GREATEST

★ Sit back and allow your foes to approach greatness. When you eventually take them down you'll inherit all that they've achieved. And apparently the bigger they are, the harder they fall.

★ Let some of your other foes fight each other, then you won't have to.

CHAPTER 7
GENIUS DELIVERED
★ The Rumble in the Jungle ★

Many are loved or hated. Ali was both. The same journalists that called him a big mouth were infatuated by his style and captivated by his non-stop chatter. He always gave them something to write about.

Ali's preparation for the George Foreman fight was a reality TV series at its very best, 30 years ahead of its time. In one memorable session, while preparing for the 1974 fight with George Foreman, Ali was drawing his workout to a close, although, for those watching, it was just getting started.

Skipping and talking, skipping and talking, his toned body bounding the metronomic beat of his rope and giving the scribes all the fodder they needed.

"Sticking. Keep dancing and sticking," pronounces Ali, amid the breathing of an athlete at work. Momentarily, while clasping the rope, he brings both hands together, crossing them briefly like the great Sugar Ray Robinson had done before him.

"Sticking. Beat him all night. Tire him out by seven rounds. He won't be so game in seven rounds."

"Right! Bring him home," chirps Bundini Brown who follows Ali around like a puppy tending to his every need; his support cast in this consuming live performance of athleticism and showmanship.

"I'm gettin' my legs ready," Ali continues. "I'll be dazzling all night. The fastest heavyweight of all time. Fastest with the rope."

Instantly Ali doubles the intensity of his workout, swinging the rope beneath his feet twice between every jump. "Time!" shouts Brown as the three-minute session comes

"Sticking. Beat him all night. Tire him out by seven rounds. He won't be so game in seven rounds."

"The stage is set for me to be ranked as the greatest of all time."

"You've been watching me train, you've been watching me dance and I look better than I did ten years ago."

to an end. Simulating a fight, Ali works for three minutes and rests for one. He hands the rope to Brown and begins circling his fitness apparatus as the world's press stand, pens poised, realising he's on a roll and waiting for more rhetoric, as Ali catches his breath.

He stops and looks back, raising his hand. "The stage is set for me to be ranked as the greatest of all time." He circles again, breathing hard and healthily, beads of sweat all over his body and face, but stops once more to continue: "Ain't no way they're gonna have no excuses after this. I've got 'em cornered. I've got the world cornered." He rounds the apparatus with Brown tracking two paces behind.

Referring to Foreman: "This is the hardest hitter since Marciano. This man's greater than Joe Louis. I've been reading what you're saying."

He wipes his brow, continuing to circle.

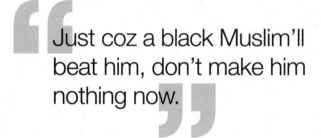

> Just coz a black Muslim'll beat him, don't make him nothing now.

Still tracking Ali, Brown laughs, almost to himself but everyone can hear. Back they come around the apparatus towards the press corps.

"He should have waited three more years. Maybe in three more years, I may have slowed down a little. But don't you believe that brainwash stuff." Ali stops walking and faces the throng and raises his hand with an accusatory finger.

"You've been watching me train, you've been watching me dance and I look better than I did ten years ago."

"Right!" echoes Brown.

Ali circles backwards, so as to face the press as he preaches.

"Don't talk all that stuff about my legs are gone. I wanted to train 20 rounds today but they won't let me."

"That's right!" says Brown.

Ali changes direction and walks straight towards the press.

"They said I was 240 at one time. They said I was fat. Look at me now," he purrs, raising his arms and looking down at his taut stomach, then to his right bicep, followed by his left.

"Don't tell me that ain't a perfect specimen of a man."

The press corps chuckle, grateful for the sparkle in Ali's eye, easing what had been a tongue-in-cheek assault aimed directly at them. The chuckles turn into loud, appreciative laughter and then applause as Ali poses for them, sweat making his body glisten like a buffed automobile. Everyone is on his side now. Captured in his charisma, travelling fast and free on his bandwagon.

"Look at that body! Slim trim and on mah toes!" Ali's voice suddenly receives an injection of energy, now fully recovered from his skipping exertions. He starts to dance, brings up his fists and shadow boxes.

"I'm on my toes now. I'm on my toes!"

The show seems to end as the photographers crowd his space to get the shot they want of Ali dancing, sticking and moving. But the show is only just starting.

Ali brings in one of his giant sparring partners, employed to mimic Foreman in every way.

"See, this man's big. This man's difficult. You build it up like George is this size. George is small. I'm as big as George or bigger. My reach is longer, my fist is bigger." For a moment the rhetoric becomes fanciful. But Ali is irresistible. He carries you with his words. With measured progression his voice gets louder, more forceful. The twinkle in his eye shines brightest when he knows, that you know, he's taking you for a ride.

The entertainer.

But then he reels himself in. The hyperbole goes and he gets down to business.

"Quit talking all this crazy talk. All these people talking about how big George Foreman is, how terrible. That I'm scared, I'm scared for my life; how relentless he is. That sucker ain't nothing. Wait till he comes in there after me. He'll fight like a damn woman. He'll hit people when they're down. The sucker's slow, he ain't got no rhythm."

Ali then morphs into a Frankenstein-like monster with awkward movement and bulky stature, showing up Foreman's lack of mobility and speed both in mind and body. Louder than before, the media men lap up his charade with raucous laughter.

Foreman, per Ali's impersonation, becomes grotesque. Frightened by the media's loud cackling, the confused monster recoils at every noise, unable to focus on one thing, drowning in a pool of distraction and fear.

Ali stops, taking a towel, his body language signalling the show is over, but there are still microphones being thrust under his nose.

> I had to trick him into this fight. I had to make the world think my legs were gone. Then they signed. They said, 'Well if he was the Ali who beat Liston, he'd beat him silly, jab him silly and dance all night. But he can't dance no more. Previous fights show that he stands in the corner.

He opens his eyes wide and bites his bottom lip, intimidating an unidentified journalist for between two seconds and an eternity, in an intoxicating mixture of fear and comedy.

"I did that on purpose man!"

Ali stops, taking
a towel, his body
language signalling
the show is over,
but there are still
microphones being
thrust under his nose.

"Can you dance?" asked the writer.

"Can I dance!?" Ali snapped back, his eyes even wider than before.

"Is the Pope a Catholic?"

Brown leads the laughter as Ali gestures to leave before turning back briefly to embolden his response, eyes bulging.

"Is you coloured?"

The scribes break into unfettered laughter. They've held court with the world's greatest entertainer and have stories for the ages to fill their pages.

Show over. But the real show was just beginning.

In Norman Mailer's book *The Fight* he gives Foreman's response to a reporter's question about whether Ali's remarks bothered him.

"No. He makes me think of a parrot who keeps saying, 'You're stupid. You're stupid.' Not to offend Muhammad Ali, but he's like that parrot. What he says, he's said before."

It has gone down in history as the most surprising, astute and original tactical approach to a boxing match of all time. What do you do against a formidable giant who, with a single blow, can lift a heavyweight champion's feet off the canvas?

You have speed and you have movement, but your aging body and the heat of the African continent mean you can't rely on that for 15 rounds.

You have charisma and support from the locals at ringside, but a booming Foreman fist won't render that an advantage for very long.

You have the resolve and courage of a lion, but there's a fine line between bravery and stupidity.

The key to Ali's approach was so ingenious that it wasn't even recognised by some of the most experienced pundits until the fight was over. Indeed many mistook Ali's tactics as further evidence that his body had depreciated, making it just a matter of time before Foreman would land the haymaker to end a great career.

Ali's ploy would come to be known as 'rope-a-dope'.

Before the fight, Norman Mailer quotes former champion Archie Moore: "I was praying, and in great sincerity, that George wouldn't kill Ali. I really felt that was a possibility."

As they came together in mid-ring for the referee's instructions, Foreman seemed void of emotion, rock-solid still. Only his eyes moved, side to side, following Ali who was full of energy, constantly jabbering through his gum shield, distracting George, chipping away at his psyche and trying to mess with his mind.

Back to their corners, the seconds cleared the ring. Now it was just the two of them and referee Zack Clayton. Foreman looked across the ring, flat footed until he could resist his nervous energy no more, turning to his corner with his hands on the ropes he leaned forward at the waist stretching his hamstrings and chest. Ali was quite a contrast floating beautifully from one foot to another, throwing loosening punches out into the early-morning air, pausing only for a brief prayer.

As the bell rang, Foreman was slow to turn and face the centre of the ring. By the time he had, Ali was already halfway across it. They both faked punches and withdrew. Almost immediately the early pattern of the fight was set. George shuffled forward in small but purposeful invasions into Ali's space, trying to cut off the ring and limit Ali's movement. Ali was bouncing, dancing, circling. As Ali's shoulders brushed the ropes — the first indication that his movement was being restricted — he landed with the first punches of the fight. A pitti-pat left hook, thrown more as a distraction to the solid right that followed up. Flush, on Foreman's jaw. The champion's instinct was to grab Ali and pull him in, removing any leverage that Ali would have to follow up and provide the respite he needed to clear his head. Ali bit hard on his gum shield and wriggled free but remained cautious, resisting the temptation to go for the kill and perhaps exhaust himself at such an early stage.

Despite this, Ali was the one throwing punches. Going backwards, circling. His next few salutations were non-scoring, brushing Foreman's gloves. But with only 30 seconds gone, and Foreman carrying his left hand negligently low, Ali landed again. This time, because they didn't land in a blurring flurry, the punches were more visible to the crowd. A single, clean right followed by a left, had the crowd on their feet, roaring for an early Ali victory. Foreman, having had time to brace for the punch, wasn't as stunned as before and he pursued the floating, retreating Ali.

Backed into a corner again, this time Ali performed an old trick, one that would earn its spurs in Zaire. As Foreman moved forward to pound the body, Ali would cuff his left hand around Foreman's neck, pulling his head down, nullifying the attack. This was the referee's signal to break the fighters, pushing George back.

Back in ring centre, Ali connected with another one-two but again refused to tire himself, grabbing Foreman's neck once more. An early pattern was developing: Bang bang from Ali, have Foreman move into range then hold and nullify until the referee called break.

Getting punched was bad enough but to then have his arms tied up when trying to retaliate became frustrating for the huge man.

With one minute, 40 seconds left in the first round, Foreman's frustration erupted. A huge, arcing, swinging left jammed into Ali's right hand, raised at the last second to protect his exposed jaw. Enthused by the roar of a crowd who thought the shot had landed, Foreman planted his feet and swung his left again, this time from behind his torso and with even greater gusto than before. Strength it had, momentum it had, but it was also telegraphed. Ali had seen it coming before the forward thrust had even been made. With the most economical of movements, Ali leaned back just enough to make Foreman hit the humid Zaire air and nothing more. To Ali, it must have been as if the world was moving in slow motion, instead of with the force and unmistakable power that only Foreman could muster.

As the punch missed its mark, Foreman's considerable momentum had him falling hazardously towards Ali.

That left-hand-around-the-back-of-the-neck ploy could therefore be upgraded to a full headlock now. The referee pulled them apart again. Foreman's frustration and perhaps the first signs of defeat became apparent. He gazed at Ali, before raising his hands in anger again.

Forward he came once more. Bang bang — hold and nullify — break.

Undeterred, onward came Foreman again. This time before Ali threw, very briefly and for the first time, Ali widened his eyes and gave a fake wobble, sarcastically pretending to be hurt. Foreman wasn't having that and threw punches again. But this time more easily than at any stage so far, Ali smothered the attack and again pushed the champion's head down until Clayton's intervention. Approaching the final minute, there were already signs that Foreman was tiring from throwing and missing, having Ali lean on his neck and being hit so often.

It was time for Ali's trademark. Many thought Ali's jab would be employed in the first few seconds but it took 104 seconds for that first jab to be flicked out, just short of the target, as Ali went backwards towards the ropes inviting Foreman in. The champion was looking ugly now. His punches lacked finesse, those big powerful arms being caught in the mesh of Ali's defence.

But with 50 seconds to go, on the ropes, Ali took a shot to the head and another. Ali's left hand was back on Foreman's neck but this time Foreman used the position to target Ali's body. If Ali was to use these tactics it was inevitable that he'd be hit downstairs and this is where his durability and tenacity, borne from the fights with Joe Frazier, would be tested again.

Clayton pulled them apart, but as they got tied up again, Foreman pounded Ali's body once more. Foreman was on top now, throwing punches upstairs as they mutually released without Clayton's intervention.

With 18 seconds left, Ali came back. Right, left — right, left. The pendulum had swung again, such that Ali could make sure the round was his on the judges' score cards. Foreman had been the one coming forward but Ali had controlled the fight and landed more blows.

Joe Frazier was sitting at ringside with British television journalist David Frost. Having lost to both fighters in the space of a year, he had numerous axes to grind and called the round even.

As the minute's rest frittered away, Ali rose from his stool and pumped his hands to the beat of the crowd's chant: "Ali, Ali, Ali." Across the ring, Foreman withdrew eye contact and focused instead on what his corner had to say.

The second round saw Foreman force the issue after realising that the pattern of the first round hadn't favoured him. They exchanged flurries with no real connection as Ali swayed out of range with his back on the ropes. As they broke and crossed the ring, Ali winced from a crushing left to his body. They broke and came together again. Precisely 30 seconds into the round, a rod-like Foreman jab was followed by a strong right hand. It looked

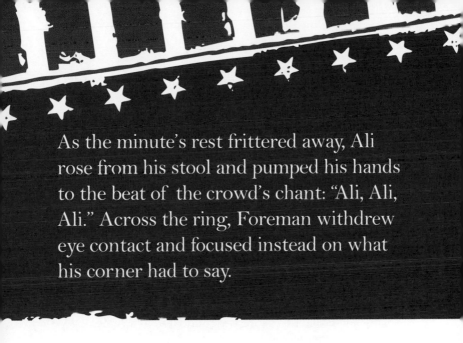

As the minute's rest frittered away, Ali rose from his stool and pumped his hands to the beat of the crowd's chant: "Ali, Ali, Ali." Across the ring, Foreman withdrew eye contact and focused instead on what his corner had to say.

more damaging than it was. Ali's cat-like reflexes turned his head away from the punch, negating much of its power. For the next minute, Foreman was the steady aggressor, landing infrequently but catching the judges' attention.

Cornered, under pressure but evading significant punishment, Ali threw three of the best left jabs of his career. Two seconds apart, each made a clear popping noise as they landed on Foreman's nose and lower forehead. Watching on video today, the only clear way to see them is to focus on Foreman's face as the punches are about to be thrown, for Ali's hand speed remains unmatchable for a heavyweight to this day.

For the next 30 seconds, Foreman tried to jab but although it sometimes landed, Ali took away the bite by leaning back, avoiding the most powerful point of its trajectory. So, Foreman changed gear, swinging wildly but landing punishing blows to Ali's sides. Quickly and predictably,

Foreman tired of these tactics in the African heat and Ali catapulted off the ropes to land a crisp left-right.

Ali made Foreman miss and countered with a magician's timing. He was talking to Foreman, knowing that the bell was coming soon. On the ropes, a swinging Foreman left came through from far back in the night air. Effortlessly, Ali swayed out of range on the ropes. Shaking his head and playing to the crowd, Ali tied Foreman up with that left hand on the giant's neck, dismissing his opponent's attack as child's play. The bell for the end of round two sounded. Foreman turned his back on Ali and walked to his corner. Ali watched him walk and shook his head dismissively again, driving the crowd wild.

Frost urged Frazier to score the round and again Joe refused to give it to Ali.

"I thought that the round was close. A very close round," he said, before becoming the first to publically misunderstand Ali's improvised rope-a-dope tactics. It wasn't just Foreman who was being made to look like a chump.

"He's hurting him, to the body. He shouldn't stay on that rope."

"Do you think Ali is making a mistake tactically every time he does that?" asked Frost, not a boxing expert but one of the best observers and reporters that the world has known.

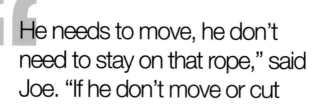

He needs to move, he don't need to stay on that rope," said Joe. "If he don't move or cut

George, George'll walk him down. He needs to move. He don't need to stay on that rope. "

Frost then turned to Ali's friend, former American football star Jim Brown for his interpretation.

"Muhammad Ali is punching George Foreman even though he's on the rope. He is getting some tremendous blows in and at some point that can tell on Foreman."

Many, like Frazier, had been conned by Ali. But others, like Brown were seeing a plan — apparently made on the fly — come to fruition. Foreman was seeing and feeling it clearer than anyone.

Round three took a now familiar shape. Foreman pressed, waiting until Ali was against the ropes and unable to retreat further. Occasionally his punches would land with force, but more often deflated only by Ali's head movement, timed to take the sting from their violence. Back Ali would come with eye-catching left-right combinations, bringing the crowd to their feet. Midway through the round, a straight right-left hook combination had the crowd wild with expectation. These were energy-sapping punches to take but Foreman wasn't desperately shaken and kept driving forward, though his work was becoming uglier.

Ali taunted his man in the clinches, talking directly into his ear. Foreman celebrated the final half of the round with a swinging four-punch combination to Ali's sides. He followed it up with a six-punch effort, five of which landed.

Moments later a couple of right hands landed on Ali's face. Heavy blows, landing with pace, that didn't rock Ali but forced him to clinch and buy some time.

Foreman saw a chance and Ali was forced to spend the next 40 seconds concentrating on defence. Foreman was making his biggest impact on the fight but as the final 10 seconds counted down, Ali snapped back with a left-right-left salvo, catching the judges' eyes and bringing Foreman back down to earth. Three seconds remaining: left-right. Two seconds: left-right. Clinch. Bell.

The referee jumped between them. Foreman glared menacingly and Ali glared back with comic ferocity. If Foreman hadn't been so recently humiliated by Ali's genius, he would surely have chuckled, along with everyone else. Whether Joe Frazier was laughing isn't clear, but he did at least now seem to understand how the fight was playing out.

"I would say George is rushing himself too much. He needs to take his time," he told Frost, acknowledging that Ali had won the round. "As time goes by, things will tell on him."

Sixteen seconds into the fourth round and a single left jab from Ali, like the three he'd thrown in round 3, landed crisp and clean. Moments later a right-left-right combination staggered Foreman, forcing him to come inside to take cover. It was the left hand that had landed the heaviest and ringside commentator Jim Sheridan noted that it was probably the hardest Foreman had been hit since Gregorio Peralta had opened a cut around his eye in the first of their two fights, almost five years earlier.

Puffiness was forming beneath the champion's right eye. The pattern of the first three rounds was now being caricatured in the fourth. Ali was picking Foreman off more frequently now and with heavier blows, yet when on the defensive, he would lean even further back over the top rope, covering up with fists over his face and forearms protecting his body. In the centre of the ring, Foreman was head hunting but off target. He would connect to the body, but the act of chasing and throwing at Ali seemed just as tiring for Foreman as it was for the challenger to absorb his blows. Ali was controlling the clinches, spinning Foreman to disrupt his balance and even pushing him away, creating enough distance and therefore leverage to land his own blows. Foreman's punches were now so ponderous that Ali, who had evaded most of the earlier bombs, could now avoid almost everything, either with upper body movement or a well-placed arm or glove.

In the final 10 seconds, the hard-working referee broke the fighters again. Ali lapsed back onto the ropes and Foreman came in swinging with a mighty left hand to the body, following up with a heavy-looking left hook to the head. This was a punch that might have taken another fighter out. Unlike so many that Foreman had thrown upstairs, this one connected. What saved Ali remains something of an enigma. He had the time and reflexes to tuck in his jaw so that the blow landed high on his forehead.

Such a blow can still knock a man out and it's difficult to see how this one didn't have more impact. It might have caught some glove on the way in and it might have made more of a glancing contact than the footage from two different angles show. It could also be that, as is widely believed, Ali had an excellent "chin", and was simply able to absorb punches to the head extremely well. That bludgeoning left remains the most mysterious punch of the fight and adds to the legend of Ali's performance. Unfazed, he avoided the follow-up swinging hook with consummate ease and seconds later connected with a blistering left-right of his own as the bell rang.

During the break, Frost asked John Daly, one of the men responsible for putting the fight together, for his thoughts. His response was prophetic:

> Ali is winning it all the way for me and I think he's going to win it within another four rounds.

As the bell rang for the fifth, Ali took two short paces from his corner and as Foreman made his way across the canvas with more positivity, Ali retreated. The challenger spent the entire first minute of the round with his back on either the ropes or corner post. Foreman landed heavily on Ali's body several times. It was only after those first 60 seconds that Ali threw anything meaningful. A jab to the body followed by a slick left hook to the base of Foreman's jaw, just below the ear. This wasn't as snappy a blow as some he'd landed but it was the only head shot that either man had landed in the round — eye-catching for the judges, clean and crisp.

Ali spent the whole of the second minute with his feet flat, shoulder-length apart, covering up and letting Foreman wear himself out. The champion's blows were wild now, thrown in huge, readable arcs. But they were fatigued, sluggish and although Ali's sides were certainly being bruised, nothing was connecting upstairs. Ali's gloves protected his face while his forearms stayed locked to his torso, limiting whatever damage Foreman could cause downstairs.

For activity alone, this was shaping up as a clear Foreman round. He could throw bombs without having to worry about defence. Ali hadn't looked in any danger but he wasn't throwing enough punches. But all the while, Ali was talking to Foreman, picking at his focus, destabilising his mind.

With 30 seconds left, Ali came off the ropes and finally threw some leather. They were peppering shots first to get his range and see how Foreman responded. Then he stepped it up, coming forward so that Foreman had no choice but to back off. Ali fired that rocking jab he'd landed earlier, right between Foreman's eyes. He missed with a follow-up left and right but as Foreman swayed from the earlier impact, he walked straight into a carving left hook from the challenger. Quickly, Ali sent over a right hand to double the champion's anguish. Jim Sheridan at ringside upped the volume of his commentary but it was no good. Drowned out by the ringsiders who were now roaring on their feet, he could not be heard. Like a redwood tree with the newly-sprouted legs of Bambi, Foreman staggered. His brain was somehow still engaged and into Ali's clutches was the only way to go. Retreat and Ali would follow and finish him, only the best boxers with feline balance can box effectively going backwards. So, in he went looking to clinch but throwing his haymakers all the while, just in case one connected. An Ali left-right caught him coming in, but still Foreman looked for cover inside. The crowd's volume was deafening now. Whatever Sheridan was yelling into his lip microphone appeared as hazy to the worldwide audience as Foreman's head must have felt.

George swung with a left hand from so far back that it almost caught referee Zach Clayton standing behind him and to the left. To almost comical effect, Ali swayed back from the neck up and avoided the blow. But it had been all-or-nothing for the champion. His momentum propelled him forwards like a toddler taking his first desperate steps, falling into the arms of his mother with outstretched arms ready to save him. And save him Ali did, tucking Foreman's head under his left arm, trapping the giant junior beneath his armpit, helpless and humiliated. Ali didn't hold back. His eyes and mouth opened wide playing to his adoring crowd. The referee wasn't going to have his ring turn into a circus and pulled the fighters apart. Just as they were heading for the next much-anticipated set to, the bell for the end of the fifth sounded a temporary halt.

Finally, Sheridan's voice could be deciphered: "By far the best round of the fight!"

The humidity of an impending thunderstorm in Zaire had loosened the ring ropes and in between rounds 5 and 6, officials made an attempt to tighten them up. Ali's trainer Angelo Dundee erupted. Like everyone else he was watching his guy's rope-a-dope tactics unfurl and knew that the loose ropes were key to letting his man sway out of range when Foreman swung upstairs.

The screaming back and forth continued as the sixth round got underway with Ali leaning over a top rope that was anything but taut. But to everyone's surprise, Ali came off the ropes and stood with Foreman. On 37 seconds he pumped that solid, fast left jab onto Foreman's chin. Bang! Another landed in that favoured spot between the eyes. Bang! And another, in exactly the same place. Ali was spending much more time off the ropes now. When Foreman threw, Ali knew his punches were weak, barely worth the effort.

His momentum propelled him forwards like a toddler taking his first desperate steps, falling into the arms of his mother with outstretched arms ready to save him.

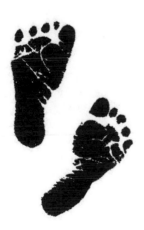

The second minute seemed to signal time off for both men. Ali rarely threw anything, taking his rest, using the ropes once more. Foreman really should have taken a leaf from the challenger's book. All his punches did was advertise his exhaustion. The first true signs that Ali's control of the fight would endure were coming now. At this rate, he could toy with the champion.

In the final 15 seconds, Ali caught Foreman with clean right hands to the head. But they were arm punches, no power was converted from turning his body into the punch. The signs were there though — Foreman could be hit, almost at will, and when he was, he refused to revert to defensive mode. All Foreman could think of now was throwing punches at his foe, but his armoury was gone, like a wounded soldier wading through a muddy field, he was sluggish and heavy-limbed.

After landing five punches to end the round — that were more like congratulatory pats on the back — Foreman turned and gasped for air, trying to fill his lungs with fuel. This was a 15-round contest and we weren't even half way through. Doom overwhelmed Foreman's gate as he turned in search of his stool. A minute's respite was all he would get. It wouldn't be enough.

The seventh started precisely as the sixth had ended. Foreman walked in, moving his arms and fists in Ali's directions; rarely could they be called punches. Head down, looking at the canvas, he was throwing only in Ali's general realm now. It seemed as if Foreman was too embarrassed to make contact. Not Ali. He was taking in every weary movement, looking for his opportunity.

Ali was off the ropes now, in the centre of the ring and boxing on retreat. Foreman was spent and as he trudged forward, Ali picked him off with trademark right-left combinations, each time studying his man for a reaction, looking for the blow that would turn the corner and allow him to press down hard on the accelerator.

Just before the two-minute mark, Foreman chased Ali across the ring, landing a clean but powder-puff left cross. The momentum of his effort forced him into a forward moving cheque that his feet couldn't cash. Into his opponent he fell, putting as much pressure on the slack ropes as they had been designed to hold. Ali, still extremely alert, rolled his man and as Foreman was now bent over forwards from the waist, Referee Zach Clayton saved the fight from an ignominious end. The champion was angling headfirst for a disastrous fall between the second and third ropes. A man of his bulk would very likely have damaged himself so much that he couldn't have continued. But Clayton, a big fellow, raced in from several steps away and tucked his right arm under Foreman's rib cage, hoisting him up and pushing him away from Ali's clutches.

Here, perhaps, Ali got cocky. He flicked out two jabs and then moved back to the ropes so that Foreman could continue to wear himself out. George swung in a left hook but kept his hand where it had landed. He moved it around to Ali's neck and as had been done to him all fight, pushed Ali's head downwards. Momentarily, as he was dragged off balance, Ali's hands came apart, his defence lax for a rare moment. From well down below his waistline, Foreman brought up an explosive uppercut to Ali's jaw. The impact rattled Ali's head — which had been angled towards the canvas — upwards and above Foreman's crouched stance. Like a beacon, Ali's handsome face was lifted high for those even in the back rows to see. The punch had landed cleanly and hard, belying the strength that we imagined Foreman had in reserve. For the briefest of moments the pro-Ali crowd fell silent, followed by awestruck oohs and ahhs.

To the amazement of anyone who watches the replay over and over again, Ali seemed unaffected, using the ropes to remain steady. To the millions watching live, his reaction stole Foreman's thunder completely. Even the eagle-eyed Sheridan was relatively underwhelmed:

> **There's a good right uppercut, thrown by Foreman – the best punch he's thrown in a couple of rounds.**

And that was that. The best single punch of the fight had gone by almost unnoticed. With 45 seconds left, in front of the watching world, Ali gathered his senses with the deception of a master criminal. Nobody could tell he was hurt, despite the inevitable ringing in his ears. While the whole episode glossed over those watching like a passing cloud, the realisation for Foreman must have been stark. At the most arduous moment of his career, he'd mustered a world-class punch from the bowels of his desperation. And yet this man, who mocked him, talked to him in clinches and embarrassed him with impudent speed was still standing, seemingly none the worse for wear. If anything destroyed Foreman that night, it was this — a punch he had thrown.

After ten seconds of head-clearing movement, Ali had the temerity to throw out six, flicking, harmless jabs, winning back the crowd's attention. Foreman came forward as

For the briefest of moments the pro-Ali crowd fell silent, followed by awestruck oohs and ahhs.

pathetically as he'd ended the previous round. Heavy armed. Heavy legged. Faltering with almighty inhalation.

The seventh ended in Foreman's corner, with Ali chattering. Both men knew that Foreman had nothing more to give. As the bell rang, they stopped punching and looked into each other's eyes. Ali moved aside and walked back to his corner. Halfway across the ring he looked back over his shoulder. It would be the last time a bell sounded to end a round in this contest.

As round eight began, Foreman had already made his way over to Ali's corner and proceeded to throw three single left hands, heavy, but lacking the snap of a fresh man. Ali, in contrast, and largely to his own poor footwork, replied with two of the crispest right hands of the night. Technically, because Foreman had circled to Ali's right and the challenger's feet hadn't compensated, Ali had become a momentary southpaw. But even that worked out for him, thanks to Foreman's now tanker-like reaction time. The first right jab was clean and halting, the second snapped Foreman's head back alarmingly.

Ali steadily turned off the ropes and retreated slowly, back across the ring. But instead of shuffling back in an orthodox stance, he paced back, alternating between orthodox and southpaw with each step. Two left hands — the first a cross shot, the second a left jab — landed with ease. The champion lunged awkwardly into Ali and squished him in the corner until Clayton drew them apart.

Ali threw a left, left-right combination in ring centre but only landed with the right. Foreman replied instantly with a scything left hand that would have taken down all the corn in Nebraska had he not been in Zaire. As a punch though, it was telegraphed, uneconomical and meat and drink for Ali, who eased back out of range before gathering his opponent's lumbering body as it fell forward. George's upper body, with the help of Ali's well-placed arm, lay uneasily over the top rope and Ali enhanced the scene by leaning on the champion's back with his forearm. It was like a man toying with a boy.

Referee Clayton again rescued the man-child and ushered him to ring centre. Swelling above Foreman's eyes was apparent now. Twenty-two minutes of exposure to Ali's cattle-rod jabs was taking its toll. Ali was playing now, his confidence high. He rocked side to side in an unfamiliar way, with both gloves at his chest. The message was that Ali could even have fun now.

For seven seconds Foreman stood in front of him, moving his hands in trepidation looking to parry blows that didn't come. Paranoia had set in.

Clayton pushed George away and realisation set in briefly. He came back in with more measure this time. Four touching but scoring left jabs landed high on Ali's face, followed by a good thudding right hand on Ali's left eye socket. This was much better work from the champion. Ali tangled with him to prevent further damage and they became mangled in each other's arms. A left-right-left from Foreman landed well. Ali had to find solace in holding and once again pushing the back of Foreman's head down with his left hand.

Again the Foreman left landed and yet again Ali tied him up. Foreman reached back to land a swinging left, but as he did, Ali popped him with a short right that threw off the champion's range, making him swing and miss.

They swung round and Foreman missed with another left as Ali found reverse gear, heading for the ropes. A follow up Foreman left did find its target.

"Again," commentated Jim Sheridan, "I caution you to look for the one punch that George Foreman can deliver at any time. This man is devastating to say the least. These punches are not, at this particular time."

Fatigue had taken Foreman's ability to turn into a punch by transferring his weight from one foot to the other, before that final movement of the shoulder. And Ali knew it.

A clumsy entanglement of arms and leather purveyed for 40 seconds. Ali was on the ropes, looking for opportunities; Foreman was leaning in, throwing weary-looking light artillery without really seeing a clear target. With Ali again holding down the champion's neck, Foreman threw ten consecutive pitty-pat alternate left and right hands to Ali's side. Ali seemed happy to let him throw. The noise level rose in the crowd. They sensed something. They were separated again but Ali stayed on the ropes.

"Maybe this could be the tactic of Ali, to let the man punch himself out. Thirty seconds left in round eight," said Sheridan at ringside. The penny had belatedly dropped.

Clayton separated them again, but Ali remained on the ropes. As Foreman came in, Ali missed with a left but landed with a speedy right hand, knocking Foreman's head sideways and up. Foreman arched forward to balance himself and Ali landed a downward arcing right to the left side of the champion's face. Again Foreman found himself leaning out of the ring over the top rope, but this time Ali didn't lean on him to exaggerate the humiliation. He threw another downward blow that landed towards the back of Foreman's ear. The champion was clear headed enough to spin himself around.

Within an instant Ali, too, had done a 180. His back was now to the centre of the ring and Foreman was on the ropes, which were just taut enough to catapult Foreman back into Ali's path, leaning forward at the waist. Ali landed a downward right, then a left-right. Flopping forward from the waist for control, before Foreman could get a sense of what was happening, Ali landed another left that brushed the champion's face, lifting it upwards. Almost before Ali could withdraw that left glove back from the target, he landed a follow up right. The speed at which it was delivered was too much to comprehend for a man on the receiving end. Foreman's arms were flailing in the wind of Ali's fanning gloves. He was dishevelled, open, exposed and wounded. Foreman's heavy left leg stamped on the canvas to absorb the blow, so heavy that he stumbled onto his right. Planting his left leg again in time to correct the collapse sideways, Foreman's upper body had folded over, forwards. As his right foot took the next compensatory step, his torso was already parallel with the canvas. His left foot came forward as quickly as his reactions could manage, desperate to neutralise a dire situation but by now his head was in freefall, his senses awash. He collapsed onto his right side and rolled onto his back. Resting up on his forearms, his right leg bent upwards at the knee. For several seconds Foreman lay there gathering his consciousness. Eventually he pulled himself up. But having got to his feet, with his gloves still pushing upwards from the floor, Clayton waved his arms, signalling the end, with two seconds of the round left on the clock.

Mailer's *The Fight* describes the immediate aftermath: "In the ring Ali fainted. It occurred suddenly and without warning and almost no one saw it. Angelo Dundee circling the ropes to shout happy words at reporters was unaware of what had happened. So were all the smiling faces. It was only the eight or ten men immediately around him who knew. Those eight or ten mouths which had just been open in celebration now turned to grimaces of horror. Bundini went from laughing to weeping in five seconds.

Why Ali fainted, nobody might ever know. Whether it was a warning against excessive pride in years to come — one private bolt from Allah — or whether the weakness of sudden exhaustion, who could know?"

"In the ring Ali fainted. It occurred suddenly and without warning and almost no one saw it."

Later that day, lounging in a robe, talking softly to filmmakers, Ali would say, "I have been boxin' for 20 years and I'm a pretty good fighter. I can walk into the firin' line with a man like Foreman and I got no fear. Nothin' can happen that I don't understand. I been to school. When he got knocked down, it was new to him and he was lost."

HOW TO BE THE GREATEST

★ Once you've allowed your foes to build a reputation, take them to the jungle and bring David Frost.

★ Survey the environment in which you operate. Analyse your opponent's strengths and weaknesses. Devise a plan that you are confident of and advise the world accordingly. If you don't feel like executing that plan on the night, just do something else. It'll work.

When you're done wiping the ring with your opponent, take an unscheduled rest on the floor. It'll probably go unnoticed.

★ THE ENTOURAGE – ANGELO DUNDEE ★

Angelo Dundee not only worked with Muhammad Ali, but also Sugar Ray Leonard and two of Ali's adversaries, Jimmy Elis and George Foreman. The Foreman relationship came years after the 'Rumble in the Jungle' but his relationship with Ellis ran concurrently with that of Ali. When the two fought to a 1971 twelfth round stoppage in favour of Ali, Dundee worked in Ellis' corner with Ali's blessing.

The Philadelphia-born trainer worked with Ali for most of his early fights and all of his contests once he came out of exile, with the exception of that Ellis fight. Among the many 'tricks' that Dundee is accused of, it's said that he loosened the ropes in Zaire so that Ali could execute the 'rope-a-dope' tactic that overcame George Foreman.

In an interview with East Side Boxing website, Dundee addressed that as a myth: "I'm going to tell you, I tightened those stinking ropes at four o'clock in the afternoon but the fight wasn't until 4am the next day. And you know what happened — the heat stretched the ropes. They were brand new hemp ropes. I didn't want those ropes to be loose. People try to say that I designed the 'rope-a-dope'. I thought Muhammad was a dope to be on the ropes. If Foreman hit him with a forearm he would have went through the ropes. That ring was like six feet up in the air — he would have broke his back, the fight would have been all over but thank God it didn't happen. He was so agile, and so quick, and so smart — he really did some good stuff."

Seventeen years later, in Leonard's famous fight with Thomas Hearns, Leonard was behind on points with all three judges after twelve rounds and suffering from a badly swollen left eye. In the corner, Dundee famously yelled at him, "You're blowing it, son!" In the thirteenth, Leonard turned the fight around, moving and forcing Hearns to move, just as Dundee had instructed. Midway through the fourteenth, the referee stopped the contest with Leonard the winner by technical knockout.

★ THE ENTOURAGE - BUNDINI BROWN ★

Drew (Bundini) Brown was also one of Ali's corner men and his assistant trainer from 1963, just prior to the Doug Jones fight in New York, until his final fight with Trevor Berbick in 1981. He's also credited with writing some of Ali's poetry, including the famous:

> Float like a butterfly, sting like a bee. Your hands can't hit what your eyes can't see.

Brown had a wild side and some ill-disciplined moments. As a Jewish man he had to tone down his drinking once the champion converted to Islam. *The New York Times* reporter Dave Anderson recalled a banquet that Ali's manager Herbert Muhammad had arranged in New York before Ali stopped Zora Folley in 1967. Bundini surveyed the scene and noted that none of the Black Muslims at the table were drinking hard liquor. So, when the waiter came, Brown leaned close and whispered, "Bring me a martini, but put it in a big water glass so nobody will know." The waiter nodded and started to walk away, but Bundini called him back and whispered in his ear, "No olive."

In the 2001 movie *Ali* starring Will Smith, in which Jamie Foxx played Brown, one scene has Ali banishing Brown from his entourage after Brown admitted selling one of Ali's championship belts on the street for $500 to feed his heroin addiction. Subsequently when Ali was training for his comeback fight with Jerry Quarry, Brown arrived at camp apparently clean of drugs and begs for his job back. The movie depicts Ali relenting by starting the "Float like a butterfly, sting like a bee" poem, only for Brown to join in with them rapping the final line in unison.

Brown died in September 1987 from what has been reported as liver and kidney complications. *The New York Times* reported that officials at the Good Samaritan Hospital in Los Angeles declined to give the cause of death.

USA Today quoted Ali as saying: "I felt like I've lost part of my body."

★ THE ENTOURAGE - DON KING ★

They say he came to Zaire with George Foreman, stepped over his beaten body seconds after Ali had knocked him out and attached himself to the new champion for the rest of his career.

Don King, who famously brushes his hair skywards from his forehead, is an opportunist, with a penchant for ceaseless chatter, greater even than that of Ali.

> I can't believe that having said what I said was interpreted as having been what I said when I said it, because I said it where I said it, when I said it, and who I said it to.

Born in 1931, the university dropout began his career in promoting boxing after convincing Ali to fight at a charity exhibition for a Cleveland hospital. It was King who promoted Ali's fight with Foreman in Zaire and the Thrilla in Manilla — the third fight between Ali and Joe Frazier.

Any fighter who was a world champion in the 1970s, '80s or '90s would likely have worked with King and a good number ended up doing so acrimoniously. Ali reportedly claimed to have been $1.2 million underpaid by King for his fight with Larry Holmes in 1980. Ali

sued, but accepted $50,000 to drop the lawsuit. Mike Tyson dropped a $100 million suit against King in exchange for a $14 million payment. Few have taken King to court and got what they asked for.

("I'm one of the world's great survivors. I'll always survive because I've got the right combination of wit, grit and bullshit.")

Outside of boxing, he also managed the Jacksons' 1984 Victory Tour and has always prided himself on the ability to make money.

("Martin Luther King took us to the mountain top: I want to take us to the bank.")

He has had several serious brushes with the law, which have involved the deaths of two men and indictments on tax evasion and insurance fraud, but frequently seems to come out relatively unscathed.

("Everything but the Lindbergh, baby." — on what the FBI was investigating him for.)

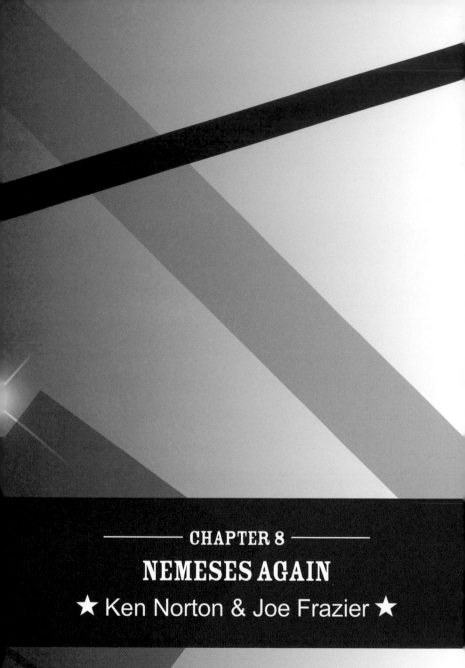

CHAPTER 8
NEMESES AGAIN
★ Ken Norton & Joe Frazier ★

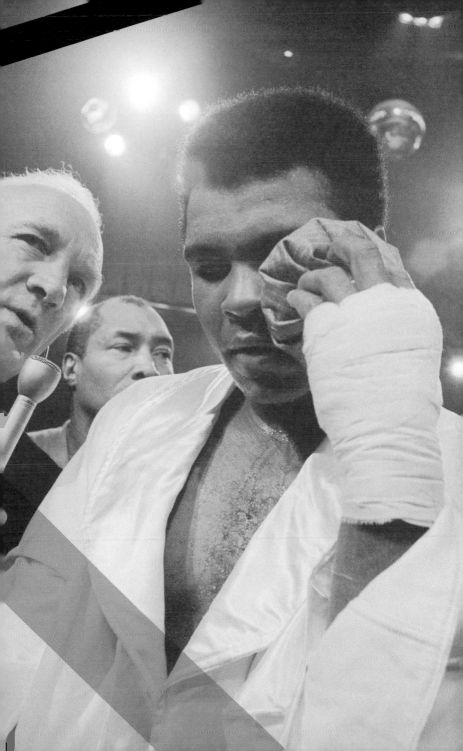

When the boxing world was clamouring for a third Ali vs Frazier fight, the economics of boxing was very different from today. Casino boxing was at an embryonic stage. Television money wasn't so dependent on location and so the live gate was the biggest factor in determining where a fight would take place. That is, unless somebody was willing to pay big money to have it in their own backyard.

As a power play in the personality cult politics of the Philippines, President Ferdinand Marcos brought the Ali vs Frazier showdown to his nation's capital, Manila. Billed as the 'Thrilla in Manila', it was also tagged, quite fittingly, as the 'Fight of the Century'.

Ali was the champion, having defeated George Foreman in the most exquisite style. Having beaten Frazier convincingly in Ali vs Frazier II and then seen Frazier get annihilated by Foreman, the Ali camp figured that Frazier was washed up. To give them both a big payday and to take advantage of the sugar daddy they had found in Marcos, Ali took the fight.

His training, though, was disrupted by an alleged affair with a woman named Veronica Porsche, who later became his wife, and it's fair to assume that Ali could have been better prepared both mentally and physically. He weighed 224 lbs for the fight, 12 pounds heavier than for Ali vs Frazier II and 8 pounds heavier than for the Foreman fight.

Come fight time, Ali was in playful mood, walking to the centre of the ring to pick up a trophy donated by Marcos for the eventual winner.

Ali's intention, according to Ferdie Pacheco, was to get the fight over quickly, inside the first five rounds. These thoughts were evident in his approach. He came out throwing punches, but not with the stylish smoothness that we'd seen before. His face was scrunched up with effort as he looked to deliver stoppage-inducing blows, rather than the scoring, hurting, wearing punches that we were used to seeing in his armoury.

Frazier was an unstoppable force of shuffling, forward momentum. No matter how much Ali threw, Frazier would not cease his advance. It became clear that this one wasn't going to end early, despite Frazier being momentarily rocked a couple of times in the first third of the 15 round fight.

As the second third of the fight wore on, Frazier's march became more targeted, trying to take Ali out with every punch he threw, pounding Ali's body, unleashing cannon balls at his head. But one of Ali's many attributes was his chin — his ability to absorb a beating without going down.

Both men were taking an enormous amount of punishment. Imagine taking a blow to the midriff. It's alarming and disarming. Ordinary men need time to recover. Ali was taking dozens of almighty 'Joe Frazier' blows in every round, but there was no chance to stop for even a brief timeout. At the same time, Ali was raining down punches on Frazier's head and something had to give. The punishment was inhuman; the intensity superhuman.

After the tenth round, with still five rounds to go, Ali went back and told his corner, "I think this is what dying is like." Never before had we seen Ali exhausted by a fighter in this way. Frazier was just as spent.

What Ali didn't know — what Frazier's corner didn't even know, with the exception of his trainer Eddie Futch — was that since a training accident in 1964, Frazier had fought with only partial vision in his left eye. Later, when asked how he'd been winning fights with only one eye, his response was: "They didn't last that long."

This fight was lasting.

The constant abuse that Frazier's face had been taking from Ali's quick hands was now starting to tell on his right eye. As that eye closed from the swelling above and below it, Frazier was now fighting the final few minutes of the contest virtually blind.

"The best in the world are getting together, and one of them is blind. You can't ignore that. You cannot ignore that," remarked Dr Pacheco, years later. "That is not only a signal of how sick the sport is, but it's a signal of how dumb Frazier is. One of the things about Frazier that nobody wants to step on, and I certainly don't, because I don't want to do anything to step on Joe Frazier but Joe Frazier was dumb."

Having boxed relentlessly all the way up to and through the thirteenth, but having taken so much punishment to the head and having had his gum shield sliced out of his mouth by an Ali right hand, Frazier's corner told him that if he didn't impress in the fourteenth round, they would stop the fight.

"Round 14 was as close as I've seen to somebody killing somebody. He was very close to killing him," remarked Pacheco in a television interview for the documentary *Thriller in Manila*.

In the same programme, Sunny Kahlid of WYPR News said of the fourteenth: "It's the most brutal of the 14 rounds that they fought. There are 5 or 6 times where Ali throws combinations where you expect Joe to fall. And he staggers. But his will keeps him up."

Ringside commentator Harry Carpenter, describing the events live: "Frazier's left eye is shutting... His mouth is bleeding... and for the first time he's looking an out-and-out loser."

Pacheco, years later:

> This is what gets people killed in boxing, where the fight becomes more important than life and death.

Frazier, years later, while watching a video of the fourteenth round:

> We were dead, both of us. I was dead. I'm fighting back but I'm fighting out of instincts.

When the bell for the end of the fourteenth rang, Ali went back to his corner and told Angelo Dundee to cut his gloves off. That was ok with Pacheco, he considered that both men were in the process of getting killed.

Across the ring, Eddie Futch had seen enough. He wasn't going to let his man suffer any further injury. Futch and Frazier, two great friends, argued about whether or not Frazier could see. According to Frazier, Futch held up his hand and said, "How many fingers?"

Frazier replied, "One."

"Ok," said Futch. "We're gonna call this off."

★ ALI VS NORTON III ★

In the period since Ali had beaten Ken Norton in their second fight, Norton had curiously got to George Foreman before Ali. It did him little good however, getting knocked out in two rounds, further building the clamour for the subsequent Ali vs Foreman clash in Zaire. Since then, Norton, aware of the huge demand for Ali's rubber match with Frazier, worked towards a similar payday for himself, notching seven straight inside-the-distance wins over a two-year period. One notable scalp was that of Jerry Quarry in five rounds, a man Ali had beaten in seven rounds three years earlier.

Having sealed his legacy and fortune against Foreman and gone through hell in the third Frazier fight, Ali was on a downward slide. He weighed as much as 230 lbs when outpointing Jimmy Young (who ended up outpointing Foreman the following year) but slimmed down to 220 for the hard-punching but outclassed Richard Dunn from England. For the third and final fight with Norton, who as always looked like Mr Universe at 217 lbs, Ali came in at a fit 221 lbs.

The fight took place at the famous Yankee Stadium in the Bronx, New York. Ali came out for the first looking a little like a baseball player in the batter's box, flat-footed with a wide stance. More side on than we'd seen him before, Ali had his weight heavily on his back foot, so as to maximise the range between him and Norton, enabling his speed of movement to traverse the chasm more quickly than his opponent.

Ali was clowning from the start, winding up the bolo punch and conducting the crowd's chants between rounds. He rode on this confidence to take the first two rounds with quick jabs and snappy right hands. In the third and fourth rounds Ali started to shuffle backwards, boxing well on retreat and taking advantage of Norton's insistence on leading with jabs to the body which left him vulnerable. Norton's swinging, somewhat telegraphed, no-look right hand was his biggest weapon in these rounds and it connected despite the big wind up, thanks to the speed at which the entire movement was unfurled.

Rounds five and six were all Norton, more because Ali allowed them to be than for any other reason. Ali wobbled ironically throughout the fifth, but the rope-a-dope tactics that worked in the African heat against Foreman weren't going to have the same impact on an athlete like Norton on a New York evening in September. The sixth saw Ali cover up in centre ring, taking the punishment almost entirely to his resistant body. But even Ali's durability winced occasionally when Norton got through with his bigger guns.

As if to show that he could dictate the pace as he pleased, Ali traded more energetically in the next two rounds. Norton's tactics didn't vary, body snatching, with his eyes down and off the target; a strong, athletic man in a boxer's uniform.

In the ninth, Ali came out dancing, landing jabs at will and nullifying Norton's oncoming style at a previously static target. As the commentators debated and even contradicted themselves as to how long Ali could keep up his fleet-footed style, one thing was certain — if he could keep this up, Norton's night was over. Although he was in great shape to go the distance, the chances of him laying an effective glove on Ali was far too rare to bother mustering hope. Norton's only chance was that Ali would be too tired to dance until the end. Sure enough Ali took a rest from his dance-floor moves towards the end of the tenth and Norton eagerly caught up with him. How would Ali approach the final five rounds, with the scorecards too close to call emphatically, one way or the other?

The eleventh round seemed to take place not in Yankee Stadium but Bizarro World. Norton applied the rope-a-dope tactic while Ali stood and threw knockout-seeking missiles. When Norton came off the ropes he threw effective jabs, uncharacteristically looking at his target as he did so. To add to the bizarre mix, it was Ali who ended up landing the heaviest punch — a straight right that knocked Norton's head back with a minute left in the round. As the bell rang, Norton spat out several words of vitriol while Ali's reply came in the form of a dismissive flicked jab to the face before both were forced to retreat to their corners.

The twelfth saw Norton continue his relentless body attack on Ali but the champion kept himself in touch with damaging flurries. It ended with Norton dabbing at his eye as if he'd been hit by a thumb. It distracted him through the minute's rest. Now we were into the championship rounds.

Thirteen and fourteen were toe-to-toe affairs characterised by Norton's hooks, mainly to the body and Ali's straight punches, mainly to the head.

The fifteenth saw Ali dancing and jabbing, rarely getting cut off and caught by Norton who was forced to eat jabs for almost the entire three minutes. Some observers will tell you that Ali's jabs in this round were powder-puff stuff and the vast majority fell short of their target. While Ali threw more punches, Norton landed more, they'll add. American television had three journalists keeping score purely unofficially, two of them called the round for Norton while the other had it even.

As the final bell rang, Ali turned his back on the fight and walked back to his corner. Norton, visibly pumped up, barked vitriol at Ali again and was lifted off the canvas by his jubilant corner men.

As the world waited for the official announcement, the pundits scoring for US TV gave in their cards. Two had it for Norton 10—5 and 8—6. Another had it level 6—6, while the co-commentator scored Norton a clear winner 9—6. When the official scores were announced, it was unanimous: 8—6, 8—7, 8—7 in favour of Muhammad Ali.

HOW TO BE THE GREATEST

★ Find that nemesis that you defeated and beat him again to avoid any doubt. Don't fight him a fourth time, there's no upside.

★ Remember Oscar Wilde: "In matters of grave importance, style, not sincerity is the vital thing." If you're struggling to beat an opponent with an ugly modus operandi, make your work look pretty. It just might be enough.

★ You can't impress all of the people all of the time. So, impress the people who matter. Television analysts don't know anything anyway.

★ YOU AGAIN? ★

Who fought the most rounds with Muhammad Ali:

1st
41 rounds

Joe Frazier

(3 fights,
Ali won 2)

2nd
39 rounds

Ken Norton

(3 fights,
Ali won 2)

3rd
30 rounds

Leon Spinks

(2 fights,
Ali won 1)

4th
27 rounds

Joe Bugner
(2 fights,
Ali won both)

George Chuvalo
(2 fights,
Ali won both)

5th
15 rounds

7 men — Ernie Terrell, Oscar Bonavena, Mac Foster, Chuck Wepner, Jimmy Young, Alfredo Evangelista and Ernie Shavers — all fought into the 15th round with Ali and lost.

★ THE BIG 4 ★

What happened when Ali, Frazier, Foreman and Norton fought each other:

1971			
Mar 8th	Frazier	W15	Ali
1973			
Jan 22nd	Foreman	TKO2	Frazier
Mar 31st	Norton	W12	Ali
Sep 10th	Ali	W12	Norton
1974			
Jan 28th	Ali	W12	Frazier
Mar 26th	Foreman	TKO2	Norton
Oct 30th	Ali	KO8	Foreman
1975			
Oct 1st	Ali	TKO14	Frazier
1976			
June 15th	Foreman	KO5	Frazier
Sept 28th	Ali	W15	Norton

★ ALI'S OPPONENTS – WHERE ARE THEY NOW? ★

Tunney Hunsaker — Career ended after a head injury put him in a coma for nine days in 1962. He suffered the physical effects for the rest of his life and was 74 when he died in 2005 after a long battle with Alzheimer's disease.

Herb Siler — Convicted for manslaughter in 1972, to serve a 7-year sentence. Upon release he owned a construction business. He died in 2001, aged 66. His grandson is NFL linebacker Brandon Siler.

Tony Esperti — Reported to have been arrested several times, ultimately sentenced for the shooting of an alleged mobster. Died in 2002, aged 72.

Lamar Clark — Died in 2006.

Duke Sabedong — A retired Hawaii State Corrections and tour industry employee, he died in 2008, aged 78.

Sonny Banks — Died in 1965 from injuries sustained in a 9-round bout.

Alejandro Lavorante — Two months after fighting Ali, he was KO'd in a Los Angles fight and died from the injuries sustained 16 months later.

Archie Moore — After an acting career, he died of heart failure in 1998 four days shy of his 85th birthday.

Henry Cooper — A television celebrity who retired to Kent, England, where he was the chairman of his local golf club, before dying in 2011.

Sonny Liston — Died in mysterious circumstances in his Las Vegas home in 1970, aged 38-42.

Brian London — A nightclub owner and fitness fanatic, London is married with three children.

Cleveland Williams — Died in a 1999 hit-and-run accident, aged 66.

Ernie Terrell — Retired in 1973 and began a career as a music producer in Chicago, Illinois

Zora Folley — Under mysterious circumstances, Folley suffered severe head injuries in a motel swimming pool while visiting a friend in Tucson, Arizona in 1972, and died within hours, aged 40.

Oscar Bonavena — Shot to death aged 33.

Jimmy Ellis — After retiring from boxing, Ellis trained boxers and worked for the Louisville Parks Department. He now suffers from dementia pugilistica.

Buster Mathis — Died aged 51, two months before his son Buster Jr fought Mike Tyson.

Mac Foster — Volunteered as a boxing coach to youths; died in 2010 aged 68.

George Chuvalo — Tours high schools speaking about the devastation of drug use to teens. Two of his sons died of drug overdoses.

Jerry Quarry — Deteriorated mentally and physically after retiring in 1992; died in hospital in 1998 aged 53. A foundation was established in his honour to battle boxing-related dementia.

Al Lewis — Became a boxing trainer in Detroit.

Floyd Patterson — Became Chairman of the New York State Athletic Commission; died at his home in New Paltz, New York in 2006, aged 71.

Bob Foster — Joined the Bernalillo County Sheriff's Department and became a detective, in the Albuquerque area.

Joe Frazier — Trained young fighters in Philadelphia and has been featured on television shows; his son, Marvin, challenged Mike Tyson for the heavyweight title. Died of liver cancer in 2011.

George Foreman — Fought on and off until age 48; is an ordained Christian minister; became well-known for the George Foreman Grill.

Chuck Wepner — Credited with inspiring the character of Rocky Balboa; Works for a wines and spirits company in Carlstadt, New Jersey.

Ron Lyle — Runs a boxing gym in Denver, Colorado.

Joe Bugner — Made failed investments in an Australian vineyard; works in the film industry and makes occasional television appearances.

Jean Pierre Coopman — Reportedly got US$100,000 from fighting Ali. Owned a bar that failed financially; has acted and paints in oil for sale.

Jimmy Young — Retired in 1988; died of a heart attack in 2005, aged 56.

Richard Dunn — Made £52,000 fighting Ali but lost more in a subsequent hotel venture; lives through the pain of an oil-rig accident in 1989.

Ken Norton — Took up a TV acting career; suffered severe injuries in a car crash; his son Ken Jr played in the NFL.

Ernie Shavers — An ordained Christian minister; now based in Liverpool, England, he works in night club security.

Leon Spinks — Keeps a low profile; voluntary worker; his son, Cory, became world welterweight champion.

Larry Holmes — Considered one of the greatest heavyweights of all time. A well-invested property owner; enjoying retirement.

Trevor Berbick — Briefly held the world title, before being knocked out by Mike Tyson; served jail time for sexual assault; killed by his nephew in 2006, aged 52, following a dispute over land.

CHAPTER 9

OLYMPIC REDEMPTION
★ The Greatest Love ★

After having won the 1960 Olympic light heavyweight gold medal in Rome, Italy, Cassius Clay returned to his home town of Louisville, Kentucky, 738 miles west of New York City.

From the late 1700s, Louisville grew rapidly as a trading centre. Cargo boats used the Ohio River as a trading route and unloaded cargo there before reaching the Falls of Ohio. The river also acted as a border between the free states and slave states and Louisville developed one of the largest slave trades in the country. The expression "sold down the river" originated as a lament for slaves, especially those from Kentucky, who were separated from their families and sold for transport down the Ohio River and Mississippi to New Orleans. Although slavery was abolished after the American Civil War in 1865, blacks still suffered from unequal opportunities, segregation and discrimination.

Clay, having won gold for his country by defeating three-time European champion Zigzy Pietrzykowski of Poland in the final, celebrated on the podium, wearing the American team's national Olympic vest. Yet back home in Louisville, having prepared hard, beaten the world's best and put his safety on the line for American Olympic glory, he was denied service in a whites-only restaurant.

The Olympic champion was so affected by this continuing lack of respect for him and his kind, that 15 years later, in his 1975 autobiography *The Greatest*, Ali tells of how he left the restaurant that day and took his Olympic medal to a bridge, before tossing it into the Ohio River. Conjecture about whether this story is true still rages. Biographers including Thomas Hauser and David Remnick have concluded that the account is untrue, that Ali simply misplaced or somehow lost the medal.

Some editors who worked at the autobiography's publishers Random House maintain that the story is untrue and was embellished. They even claim that Ali denied the account at a press conference to launch the book.

In an article at courier-journal.com based in Louisville, C. Ray Hall wrote in August 2010:

Today, Ali talks about the subject, "only if someone asks him," said his wife, Lonnie.

And if someone asks if he really threw the medal off a bridge?

"He'd say yes," Lonnie said. "And then sometimes he doesn't answer. He never says no. I've never heard him say no."

Years later Ali has related part of the story several times with good humour, as he did in this example during a sit-down television interview:

"I went downtown. At the time, black people were marching to eat in the white restaurants and they wanted rights to go where they wanted to. So I said, 'I'll take this medal and I'll go downtown and I'll set down in a restaurant. I've got them in a spot now. Then I'll order something to eat.'

And I went down, and I had my medal on and the lady was lookin'. And I said, 'I'd like a cheeseburger.' She said, 'We don't serve negros.' I said, "I don't eat 'em, just give me a cheeseburger."

Whatever the facts of the story, one thing is universally accepted — Ali no was longer in possession of the medal that propelled the most celebrated boxing career of all time. 36 years later that would be redressed.

By the time Atlanta, Georgia hosted the 1996 Olympic Games, America was a different place. Blacks and other ethnic minorities had gained greater acceptance from the mainstream, the electorate was just 12 years away from electing its first black president and Muhammad Ali was viewed in a very different light. For the most part, he was now warmly embraced and greatly loved. Over time, the Vietnam War that he refused to be a part of came to be seen as a tragedy, with Ali's stand viewed as one of the earliest stances that garnered wide-ranging empathy by those viewing it at the dawn of the 21st century.

Ali's skill in the ring could now be viewed in the context of all boxing history and his legacy as "The Greatest" was doubted by few, at least among heavyweights. His role as a loud-mouth braggart by this time was seen as ground-breaking entertainment and in the context of a man now in advanced years and failing health, somewhat adorable. In the years that followed Ali's career, many boxers tried to copy his bold ways.

No one has ever pulled it off quite in the way Ali did. It paved the way for Sugar Ray Leonard to develop his own very successful persona, but most crashed and even burned when trying to take flash, charisma and self-admiration to the Ali degree. It needed backing up with rare talent.

Global love for the man that America tried to jail and stole the best years of his career from had become unbounded and transcended the sport.

In 1974, the year he beat George Foreman, Ali was named the *Sports Illustrated* Sportsman of the Year. Across the Atlantic in the late 1970s, soccer players interviewed by the English magazine Shoot, resoundingly voted Ali the man they would most like to meet. In 1979, the Texas Southern University presented Ali with an Honorary Doctorate of Humane Letters. In that same year, a Louisville street was named after him. In 1997 he was given the Essence Living Legend Award, while ESPN presented him with the Arthur Ashe Award for Courage. In 2005, President George W. Bush presented him with the Presidential Medal of Freedom and that same year, in Berlin, he was presented with the Otto Hahn Peace Medal.

But perhaps the honour that resonates with most with Ali was at the Atlanta Olympics, when the case of the lost gold medal was visited again.

As Ali, ravaged by Parkinson's Disease and televised live around the world, lit the flame that made its way up to the Centennial Olympic Stadium torch in Hank Aaron Drive, Atlanta, American television commentators chose these words:

> **Muhammad Ali of course, an Olympian as young Cassius Clay, gold medal boxer, 1960, the Games of Rome – has become arguably the most famous person on this Earth.**

Days later at half time in the final of the men's basketball between the USA and Yugoslavia, not knowing what was in store, the crowd noticed a golf cart make its way into the arena and instantly recognised the front-seat passenger as Ali. Television announcer Bob Costas knew what was in store and explained this to the watching viewers.

As Ali was led to mid-court, the public address announcer made a statement to the live and television audience:

"The story goes that in disgust, he took off his medal and threw it into the Ohio River. That is not true, the medal was simply lost. It makes a good symbolic story, it could have happened, it actually did not. But somehow the medal was misplaced and now that situation will be rectified."

"At the 1960 Rome Olympics, an 18-year old from Louisville, Kentucky won a boxing gold medal. He was admired as an athlete and even then was also admired for his engaging personality. After Rome he would go on to a boxing career without equal."

"Also for the past 36 years he has become a worldwide symbol of hope and possibility. But an important piece of his history has been lost — the gold medal. Tonight the President of the International Olympic Committee Juan Antonio Samarach is here to present to Muhammad Ali this replacement for the boxing gold medal he won at the Games of the seventeenth Olympiad."

It was only at that moment that the live audience realised the reason for Ali's presence. They rose as one to applaud the frail, yet still handsome Ali, who's quivering hand rose in acknowledgement.

Ali accepted the medal placed around his neck, offered his hand for Samarach to shake, bent forward to kiss the President on both cheeks and lifted the medal up to his lips.

Ali, now only a fraction of the expressive man he once was, still had that glint in his eye, just as noticeable as it ever was, perhaps because everybody now searched so hard to see it. But it was there and the glint turned into an emotional smile when the US basketball team moved to embrace and kiss him and pose for photographs.

Scottie Pippen, Shaquille O'Neal, Charles Barkley and the rest of the USA's "Dream Team" were all desperate to pay their respects and become a part of this historic moment. Ali's smile was beaming now. A man so imprisoned by his restricted motor skills, he raised a hand beckoning Charles Barkley to bring his ear to Ali's lips, so that he could whisper acknowledgement. Barkley withdrew in laughter as Ali chuckled.

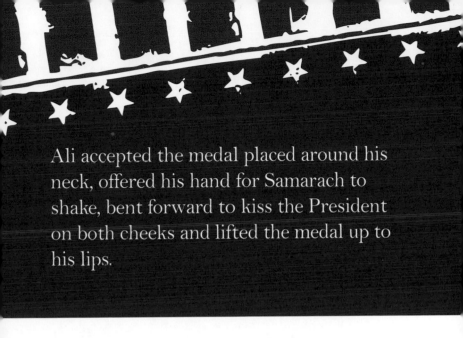

Ali accepted the medal placed around his neck, offered his hand for Samarach to shake, bent forward to kiss the President on both cheeks and lifted the medal up to his lips.

The Yugoslavian players, representing global respect for Muhammad Ali, also came to gather round Ali and show their love for the champion, posing for a photograph to seal their participation in a moment of magic.

As he was ushered away by officials for the teams to continue their warm up for the second half's action, Ali gave the crowd and television viewers the moment they had been waiting for.

Freed by love from the manacles of disease around his limbs, Ali raised both arms above his head, waved and circled. His eyes glinted, as engaging as his words once were, when he was The Greatest.

★ Stay true to your core values. Let time ease the intensity of your rivalries and become a humanitarian. When you've done your talking, listen to what is being said. Say "Thank you".

★ Accept that there may be deep scars of battle. Fighting for a cause isn't always about victory for you. There are new generations to come and they will enjoy the sweetness of your win.

★ ALI'S CAREER RECORD: W56, L5, D0 ★

———— 1960 ————

29 Oct	Tunney Hunsaker W 6 Louisville, KY
27 Dec	Herb Siler W KO 4 Miami Beach, FL

———— 1961 ————

17 Jan	Tony Esperti W TKO 3 Miami Beach, FL
7 Feb	Jim Robinson W KO 1 Miami Beach, FL
21 Feb	Donnie Fleeman W TKO 7 Miami Beach, FL
19 Apr	Lamar Clark W KO 2 Louisville, KY
16 Jun	Duke Sabedong W 10
22 Jul	Alonzo Johnson W 10 Louisville, KY
7 Oct	Alex Miteff W TKO 6 Louisville, KY
29 Nov	Willi Besmanoff W TKO 7 Louisville, KY

———— 1962 ————

19 Feb	Sonny Banks W TKO 4 New York, NY
28 Mar	Don Warner W TKO 4 Miami Beach, FL
23 Apr	George Logan W TKO 6 Los Angeles, CA
19 May	Billy Daniels W TKO 7 New York, NY
20 July	Alejandro Lavorante W KO 5 Los Angeles, CA
15 Nov	Archie Moore W TKO 4 Los Angeles

———— 1962 ————

24 Jan	Charlie Powell W KO 3 Pittsburgh, PA
13 Mar	Doug Jones W 10 New York, NY
18 Jun	Henry Cooper W TKO 5 London, UK

1964

25 Feb   Sonny Liston W RTD 7 Miami Beach, FL

1965

25 May   Sonny Liston W KO 1 Lewiston, Maine
22 Nov   Floyd Patterson W TKO 12 Las Vegas

1966

26 Mar   George Chuvalo W 15 Toronto
21 May   Henry Cooper W KO 6 London
6 Aug   Brian London W KO 3 London
10 Sept   Karl Mildenberger W TKO 12
                  Frankfurt, Germany
14 Nov   Cleveland Williams W TKO 3 Houston, TX

1967

6 Feb   Ernie Terrell W 15 Houston, TX
22 Mar   Zora Folley W KO 7 New York, NY

1970

26 Oct   Jerry Quarry W TKO 3 Atlanta
7 Dec   Oscar Bonavena W TKO 15 New York

1971

8 Mar   Joe Frazier W L 15 New York
26 Jul   Jimmy Ellis W TKO 12 Houston, TX
17 Nov   Buster Mathis W 12 Houston, TX
26 Dec   Jurgen Blin W KO 7 Zurich, Switzerland

1972

1 Apr	Mac Foster W 15 Tokyo
1 May	George Chuvalo W 12 Vancouver, BC
27 Jun	Jerry Quarry W TKO 7 Las Vegas
19 July	Al Lewis W TKO 11 Dublin
20 Sept	Floyd Patterson W TKO 7 New York
21 Nov	Bob Foster W KO 7 Stateline, NV

1973

14 Feb	Joe Bugner W 12 Las Vegas
31 Mar	Ken Norton L 12 San Diego
10 Sept	Ken Norton W 12 Los Angeles
21 Oct	Rudi Lubbers W 12 Jakarta, Indonesia

1974

28 Jan	Joe Frazier W 12 New York
30 Oct	George Foreman W KO 8 Kinshasa, Zaire

1975

24 Mar	Chuck Wepner W TKO 15 Cleveland
16 May	Ron Lyle W TKO 11 Las Vegas
30 Jun	Joe Bugner W 15 Kuala Lumpur, Malaysia
30 Sept	Joe Frazier W RTD 14 Manila, Philippines

1976

20 Feb	Jean Pierre Coopman W KO 5 San Juan, PR
30 Apr	Jimmy Young W 15 Landover, MD
24 May	Richard Dunn W TKO 5 Munich, Germany
28 Sept	Ken Norton W15 New York

1977

| 16 May | Alfredo Evangelista W 15 Landover, MD |
| 29 Sept | Ernie Shavers W 15 New York |

1978

| 15 Feb | Leon Spinks L 15 Las Vegas |
| 15 Sept | Leon Spinks W 15 New Orleans |

1980

| 2 Oct | Larry Holmes L TKO 11 Las Vegas |

1981

| 11 Dec | Trevor Berbick L 10 Nassau, Bahamas |

★ WHO ELSE COULD BE THE GREATEST? – SUGAR RAY ROBINSON ★

Muhammad Ali was never backward at coming forward with his opinion of who the greatest of all time was. So much so that it forms the very title of this book. But careful and patient quizzing of Ali on the subject will clarify that his rantings on who the greatest is were confined to the heavyweight division.

'Pound-for-pound' is an expression used by boxing aficionados to equate the various advantages of fighters in different weight categories. And the question of who is pound-for-pound the greatest fighter of all time, is most frequently answered with three words: Sugar Ray Robinson. Ask Ali, ask Joe Louis, ask Sugar Ray Leonard, ask *The Ring* magazine and you'll get the same answer.

Born Walker Smith Jnr in May 1921, he amassed a perfect 85—0 amateur record. He was a beautiful boxer to watch, able to move gracefully, with speed, as Ali managed to do years later, despite being the bigger man. What Ali lacked in single-punch power, Robinson had in great supply. 69 of his 85 amateur wins had come via knockout, 40 of them in the first round.

He turned professional at the age of 19, holding the World Welterweight Championship from 1946 until 1951.

Having vacated that crown, he moved up to the 160-pound middleweight division in 1951, stopping Jake LaMotta in the 13th round, only to lose it five months later by a fifteen-round decision to British fighter Randy Turpin in London. Two months later, he won the rematch in a dramatic 10th-round knockout, despite bleeding from a cut above the left eye.

He would lose and regain the crown once more, before a 1957 loss to Gene Fullmer. But four months later he won the title for the fourth time, knocking Fullmer out in the 5th round with a perfect left hook, on a night where *The New York Times* described Robinson as "the splendid flash from Harlem". Later that year he lost the title to Carmen Basilio in a 15-round decision, regaining it in a 1958 rematch again having gone the distance, becoming the only man to win a World Title five times.

Robinson died a poor man in 1989, despite the millions he had earned in the ring. An extract from *The New York Times* obituary reads:

"'I went through four million dollars, but I have no regrets,' he once said. 'If I had the chance to do it over again, I'd do it the same way. I didn't gamble away my money. I used it to let people live. I took my family and my friends on trips with me. I loaned it to strangers to pay their bills, and sometimes I didn't get it back.'"

Of Robinson, Muhammad Ali said:

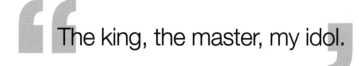

The king, the master, my idol.

★ WHO ELSE COULD BE THE GREATEST? – SUGAR RAY LEONARD ★

'Sugar' Ray Leonard was, like Ali, an Olympic gold medallist. His gong came 22 years after Ali's triumph, at the 1976 Montreal Games. Unlike Ali, he didn't come from the glamourous heavyweight division. Leonard, by comparison, was a scrawny-looking black kid fighting at light welterweight (63.5 kg).

When Leonard turned pro in 1977, the world looked at boxing quite differently than when Ali made his debut. Ali had transformed the sport into a mass market television spectacle and as a by-product, casino-staged boxing had become an extremely lucrative venture for promoters and fighters alike.

While Ali had switched on the light, he'd left the room empty by retiring. In 1977, Ali was fighting pedestrian 15-rounders with the likes of Alfredo Evangelista and the public were gagging for a new superstar. It wasn't hard to see that Ali's career was well down its final hill.

In stepped 'Sugar' Ray and by the time he had wowed the new cable TV market with his movie-star good looks, dazzling hand speed and telegenic charisma, he was ready for a title tilt. His shot at the World Welterweight title came 14 months after Ali had waved goodbye to the sport with his rematch against Leon Spinks, leaving a chasm that some thought might never be filled.

Leonard went on to make even more money than Ali, becoming the first boxer to gross more than US$100 million.

His World Boxing Association title win came against Puerto Rican Wifredo Benitez, easily one of the best pound-for-pound boxers of his era. Leonard dropped Benitez in the third round, and went on to stop him with six seconds left in the fight, ahead on all three scorecards.

From then on, Leonard transcended the sport, as Ali had, winning admirers even from those who didn't follow boxing. His first defence against Dave 'Boy' Green ended with the most devastating single-punch finish that this writer has even seen — a left hook that knocked the Brit out cold.

Then came two fights with the legendary Roberto Duran. He lost the first on points, mixing it with the Panamanian brawler, when he should have boxed. But in the rematch Duran infamously said "No mas" — Spanish for no more — as Leonard's speed and talent humiliated the champion into submission.

Leonard's impressive wins against other contenders and light middleweight champion Ayub Kalule set up a mega fight with the World Boxing Council's welterweight champion Thomas Hearns, a six-foot-two freak at 147 pounds. Behind on all three of the judges' scorecards, Leonard's trainer Angelo Dundee, who also trained Ali, famously told Leonard, "You're blowing it, son!" In the very next round, Leonard won by a knockout.

After a stuttering knockout of the mediocre Kevin Howard, Leonard retired after surgery to repair a detached retina, only to come back two years later, enticed by the prospect of meeting 'Marvelous' Marvin Hagler for the World Middleweight Title.

Behind on all three of the judges' scorecards, Leonard's trainer Angelo Dundee, who also trained Ali, famously told Leonard, "You're blowing it, son!" In the very next round, Leonard won by a knockout.

Hagler was by now arguably slowing after 12 defences, including those against Duran, Hearns and the highly-rated John Mugabi.

In a 12-round fight that thrilled from start to finish, Leonard moved, flurried and sped his way to a split decision win that is perhaps the most hotly debated verdict of all time. Despite much talk of a rematch, a surly Hagler retired never to fight again, while Leonard won the Light Heavyweight crown against Donny Lalonde, becoming a four-weight world champion — only to wane in the four remaining fights of his career, which included a draw with Hearns and another win over Duran.

★ WHO ELSE COULD BE THE GREATEST? - MANNY PACQUIAO ★

The PacMan has emerged as arguably Asia's most successful sportsman ever. It's hard to think of anyone who has earned more money or garnered more pure affection from their countrymen. Asia has supplied Formula 1 drivers, grand slam winning tennis players, English Premier League footballers, Major League Baseball starting pitchers, NBA superstars, as well many fine cricketers. But nobody currently generates as much respect on a global scale as Manny Pacquiao.

In 2008, ESPN's Asian-based cable television channel asked its viewers to vote for their Champion of Champions, essentially a popularity contest. The online votes, in their millions, saw Pacquiao triumph over idolised cricketer Sachin Tendulkar and even stars from beyond Asia such as then Manchester United footballer Cristiano Ronaldo, Formula 1 world champion Lewis Hamilton, golfer Tiger Woods and tennis players Roger Federer and Rafael Nadal.

The Filipino has won ten world titles in an unfathomable 8 different divisions. Having started his career at light flyweight (108 lbs), he has gained sufficient 'good' weight to win world titles right up to Super Welterweight (154 lbs) — and isn't done yet.

Like all greats, Pacquiao's legacy will be defined at least in part by the quality of the other fighters of his era. He beat greats Oscar De La Hoya (who was past his best) and Ricky Hatton (who was arguably at his peak) and could barely have done more than what has been asked of him.

Asia has supplied Formula 1 drivers, grand slam winning tennis players, English Premier League footballers, Major League Baseball starting pitchers, NBA superstars, as well many fine cricketers. But nobody currently generates as much respect on a global scale as Manny Pacquiao.

Like Ali, he also has key adversaries whom he's got the better of over the course of several matches and rematches — Juan Manuel Marquez, Erik Morales and Marco Antonio Barrera will forge the most enduring memories. But the fight that might clinch Pacquiao's claim to being the greatest ever, at the time of writing, has yet to be made. Floyd Mayweather, if they ever fight, will represent an opponent who is classier (in the ring, sadly not out of it) than anyone Pacquiao has fought before. Mayweather is the only other man to have beaten Ricky Hatton and has danced around a fight with Pacquaio for several years now.

The fight may never be made but if it is, the winner has every right to be included in the list of the greatest ever, pound-for-pound.

★ WHO ELSE COULD BE THE GREATEST? – HENRY ARMSTRONG ★

What makes boxing an art and its technique so important is that natural physical advantages have largely been removed. Making boxers fight within a weight limit means that one man's skill can't be obliterated by another man's size. What you make in height, you lose in breadth and thus 'all boxers are created equal'.

Today there are seventeen weight categories with as little as three pounds separating some at the lighter end of the scale. In Henry Armstrong's day there were only eight: flyweight, bantamweight, featherweight, lightweight, welterweight, middleweight, light heavyweight and heavyweight. From featherweight to welterweight, a spread of 21 lbs, 'Hammerin' Hank' not only became the first man to win World titles at three different weights, he also held them simultaneously, making more defences of the welterweight crown than any other man in history.

The eleventh child of fifteen had a perpetual 'buzz-saw' style that was too much for the best boxers of his day to handle. The historic period of his three-weight domination began on 29 October 1937, when he won the world featherweight (126 pounds) crown by stopping Pete Sarron in the sixth round. Seven months later on 31 May 1938, he moved up two classes to win the welterweight (147 pounds) title with a fifteen-round decision against Barney Ross.

Then less than three months later on 17 August 1938, Armstrong dropped weight to win the lightweight (135 pounds) championship with a 15-round split decision over Lou Ambers before a crowd of 19,216 at Madison Square Garden in New York. Armstrong had been badly cut around the eyes and inside the mouth. The referee had warned him that if the injury got worse he would stop the contest. The 25-year-old's response was to spit out his gum shield so that he could swallow the blood more easily and hide it from the referee. He would later need 37 stitches to close the wound inside his mouth.

The following year Armstrong came close to adding a fourth title, stepping up to fight a draw with Ceferino Garcia for the world middleweight crown in Los Angeles. When a championship fight ends in a draw, the champion retains his belt.

In a career of 181 fights, Armstrong won 152, winning 100 by stoppage. In 2007, *The Ring* ranked Armstrong as the second greatest fighter of the last 80 years. After retiring, Armstrong became ordained as a Baptist minister in Los Angeles. Despite collective purses exceeding a million dollars, in the final years of his life, *The New York Times* recorded that "Mr. Armstrong and his wife, Gussie, lived on a monthly US$800 Social Security check, and he suffered from a string of maladies that included pneumonia, anemia, cataracts, malnutrition and dementia."

He died in 1988.

★ WHO ELSE COULD BE THE GREATEST? - ROY JONES JUNIOR ★

When Roy Jones Jnr beat John Ruiz to win the World Boxing Association (WBA) Heavyweight Championship, he became the first former World Middleweight Champion to win the heavyweight title in 106 years. He did so, not as a natural heavyweight (he weighed 199 lbs to Ruiz's 226 lbs) but as a fighter whose skills could transcend weight divisions.

It wasn't the first time this had happened. Jones started out as a light middleweight, with a 140 lb limit, claiming his first World Championship at middleweight by beating Bernard Hopkins for the International Boxing Federation (IBF) crown in 1993. The following year, having had some non-title fights at the super middleweight limit of 168 lbs, he outclassed James Toney for the IBF title at that weight. Having defended that belt five times, he moved up again to light heavyweight and challenged Montell Griffin for his World Boxing Council belt in 1997. Jones dominated the contest and had Griffin down and almost out. But as Griffin took a knee to avoid punishment in the ninth, Jones hit him twice rather than backing off to allow a count to begin. For that, Jones lost via disqualification but in the rematch, five months later, he won in a first round knockout. In a non-title fight he beat former Light Heavyweight world champion Virgil Hill via a 4th round stoppage, then claimed the WBA version of the title in mid-1998.

Jones defended those titles, picking up several other versions of the light heavyweight crown until he conquered the heavyweight scene against Ruiz. He subsequently lost his light heavyweight titles, but at age 39 fought the unbeaten Welshman Joe Calzaghe, who according to *The Ring*, had the linear claim to the crown. As thousands of Welshmen took over New York's Madison Square Garden, this was thought to be Jones' final tilt at world glory. He looked about to claim it in the very first round when Jones dropped Calzaghe, cutting him in the process. But the Welshman got up and won convincingly, perhaps, ironically because he was carrying an injury. Though the champion threw hundreds of punches over the 12 rounds, none seemed to carry the power of his full bodyweight. Calzaghe was protecting damaged hands but in doing so, piled up the points without tiring or exposing himself. Jones was easily outscored and although he fought again, hasn't won a world title since.

George Foreman, former World Heavyweight Champion and opponent of Muhammad Ali, said that Jones hit like a heavyweight but moved like a lightweight.

Why not leave it though to one who knows as well as anyone else, one who's seen and studied all of the greats, former editor of *The Ring*, Bert Randolph Sugar.

After Jones beat Mike McCallum for the World Boxing Council light heavyweight crown in a 1996 unanimous decision, Sugar proclaimed Jones "the greatest fighter of all time".

After Jones beat Mike McCallum
for the World Boxing Council
light heavyweight crown in a
1996 unanimous decision,
Sugar proclaimed Jones
"the greatest fighter of
all time".

ABOUT THE AUTHOR

Steve Dawson is a reformed Chartered Tax Accountant, who after 10 years of battling the Inland Revenue, devoted his career to what he'd already been doing in his spare time — journalism.

He was born in 1966, in Lewisham, to parents who had grown up in the small north England village of Great Ayton. He attended school in East Anglia, Cheshire and Kent before graduating from Royal Holloway and Bedford New College, University of London, where he studied Economics and Public Administration.

A keen sports enthusiast, he once got in the ring with three-time world title challenger Herol "Bomber" Graham, but despite his opponent's hands being tied behind his back, was unable to land a punch on the middleweight's faultless features.

His first writing break came in London for the weekly paper *Boxing News*, where he introduced future world featherweight champion Colin McMillan to the mainstream.

After spending the second half of his taxing full-time career in Singapore, he decided on a mid-career change. In 1999 he joined *The Straits Times* as a correspondent. Then, having straddled the print and television media for two years, he scuttled across to the short-lived but long-loved Channel i News bulletin on a permanent basis in 2003. After anchoring the Olympic Games and UEFA European Championships coverage the following year, Steve joined ESPN Star Sports as a writer and presenter for the world-renowned nightly news show, *Sportscenter*.

While still anchoring *Sportscenter* and commentating on mixed martial arts, boxing and tennis on ESPN, Steve is now in his eighth year of presenting Formula One and also presents English Premier League football on Star Sports.

Steve is married to Diana. They have two inspiring daughters, Amelia and Haley, a rabbit named Dakota and a puppy named Roo.

PHOTO CREDITS